CW01261855

*'Auto'-Biography*

*by Arthur Knowles*
WITH CAMPBELL AT CONISTON

*by Arthur Knowles and Dorothy, Lady Campbell*
DONALD CAMPBELL CBE

ARTHUR KNOWLES

# 'AUTO'-BIOGRAPHY
## My Forty Years' Motoring

ILLUSTRATED

*London*
GEORGE ALLEN AND UNWIN LTD
RUSKIN HOUSE MUSEUM STREET

FIRST PUBLISHED IN 1970

This book is copyright under the Berne Convention.
All rights reserved. Apart from any fair dealing for the
purpose of private study, research, criticism or review,
as permitted under the Copyright Act, 1956, no part of
this publication may be reproduced, stored in a retrieval
system, or transmitted, in any form or by any means, electronic, electrical, chemical, mechanical, optical, photocopying, recording or otherwise, without the prior permission
of the copyright owner. Enquiries should be addressed
to the Publishers.

© *George Allen & Unwin Ltd, 1970*

ISBN 0 04 796035 3

PRINTED IN GREAT BRITAIN
*in 11 point Plantin type*
BY COX AND WYMAN LTD
FAKENHAM

*This book is dedicated to friends present and friends past, and to the motor car, which brought us all together*

ACKNOWLEDGMENTS

The author is greatly indebted to Arnold Bolton and Peter Garner of BLMC's *High Road* magazine for their generous help, and to the British Leyland Motor Corporation, the Montagu Motor Museum at Beaulieu and the Radio Times Hulton Picture Library, for their permission to reproduce photographs.

# CONTENTS

1. Learning the hard way — page 13
2. Sand in the 'blower' — 28
3. The 'Hyper-Leaf' — 40
4. A lap or two with Billy — 54
5. 'Miss England II' — 64
6. In which father changes course — 73
7. Roman orgy — 84
8. A pair of swallows — 99
9. The 'Tiger', the Bentley and the J.3 — 113
10. In which I change course — 126
11. Sorting the wheat from the chaff — 137
12. We take to the hills — 150

INDEX — 161

# ILLUSTRATIONS

1. *Segrave looks on as Sunbeam is prepared* — facing page 16
2. *Final adjustments* — 17
3. *General view at Southport Sands* — 32
4. *Major Segrave in Hush-Hush No. 1 at Southport* — between 32–3
5. *Major Segrave breaks world record at Southport* — 32–3
6. *'. . . and he's away'* — facing 33
7. *May Cunliffe and father at Southport* — 48
8. *Kaye Don in 'Hyper-Sports' No. 28* — between 48–9
9. *The Kay Don 'Hyper-Sports' Lea-Francis* — 48–9
10. *Motor-racing in a blizzard* — facing 49
11. *Jack Field and De Ferranti neck-and-neck at Birkdale Sands* — facing 64
12. *De Ferranti and Thompson at Southport Beach in a blizzard* — 65
13. *Dignity and impudence* — 80
14. *Moss wins 15-mile race at Southport, 1933* — 81
15. *Cornering at Southport* — 96
16. *On the banking at Brooklands* — between 96–7
17. *The Morris 'Bullnose'* — 96–7
18. *The Riley 'Monaco', 1927* — facing 97
19. *The first 'Midget', MG M-type, 1928* — 112
20. *The Austin Seven 'Swallow'* — between 112–13
21. *The MG J3-type 'Midget', 1933* — 112–13
22. *The MG TF-type 'Midget' of 1953.* — facing 113
23. *The S.S. Jaguar '100'* — 128
24. *I managed to own a '1$\frac{1}{2}$', but the '4·2' will elude me* — 129

1914

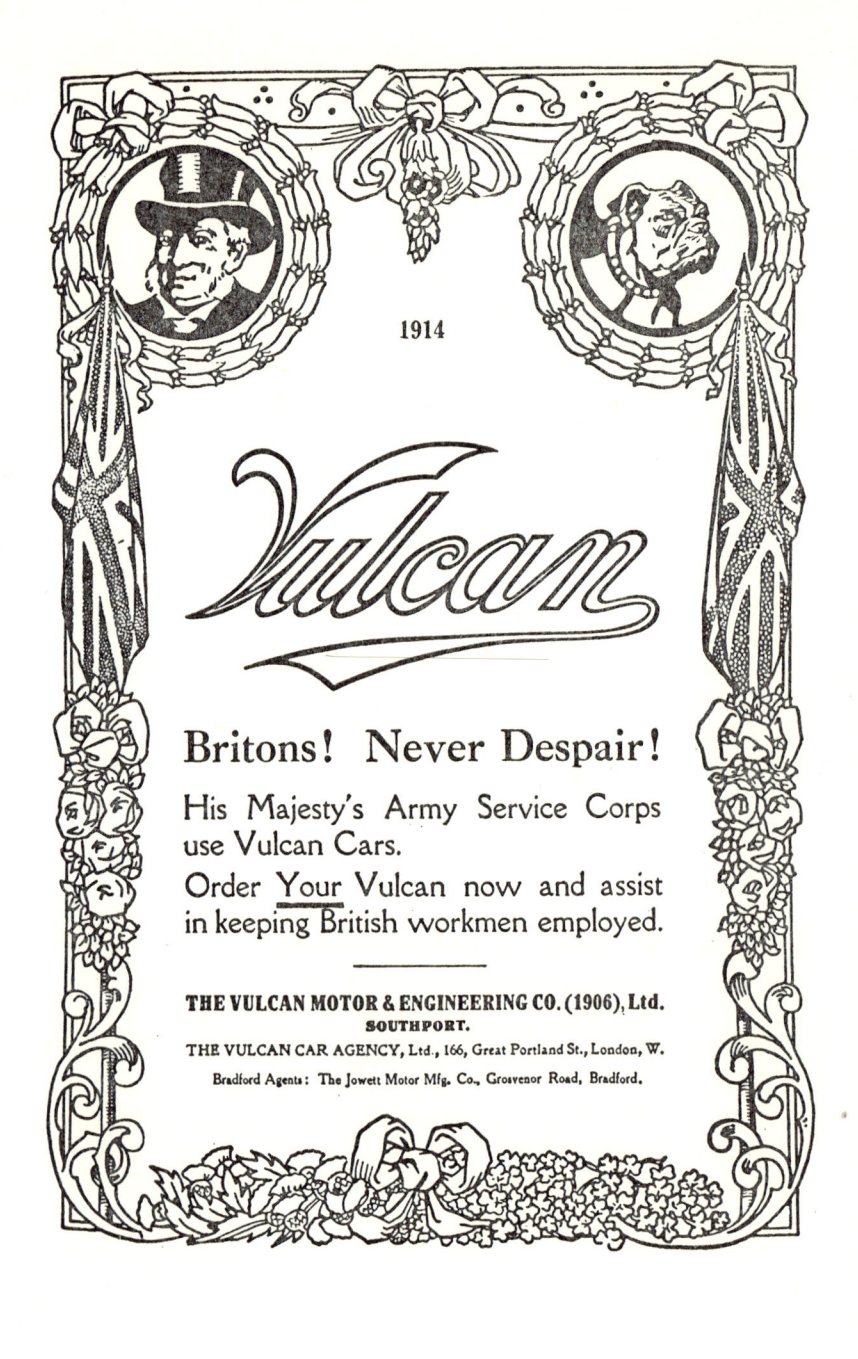

# *Vulcan*

## Britons! Never Despair!

His Majesty's Army Service Corps use Vulcan Cars.

Order Your Vulcan now and assist in keeping British workmen employed.

**THE VULCAN MOTOR & ENGINEERING CO. (1906), Ltd.**
**SOUTHPORT.**
THE VULCAN CAR AGENCY, Ltd., 166, Great Portland St., London, W.
Bradford Agents: The Jowett Motor Mfg. Co., Grosvenor Road, Bradford.

CHAPTER ONE

# Learning the hard way

I suppose it was inevitable that either my brother Tommy or I should become obsessed with cars, in one way or another. We both became deeply involved in matters motoring at a very early age, and I should not have been surprised to learn that we were weaned on a mixture of petrol and oil or that we cut our teeth on piston rings. As it transpired, I was the one to fall for the car, hook, line and sinker, Tommy coming to regard it merely as a means of transport, a necessary accessory to his way of life, and caring little for the manner by which it was propelled, or in 'getting underneath to fix it'.

My father was responsible, for in the early 1900s he became dissatisfied with his job in a Lancashire factory with which his family was closely associated, and which specialized in making textile machinery. He sought wider fields and greater scope for his rapidly developing skills in both engineering design and practice, for to him textile machinery was boring, its design too static, modification minimal and improvements slow to materialize. There was for him too little opportunity for creative work, so his search and a growing interest in motor transport took him to Southport, the seaside town on the Lancashire coastline. There, in the village of Crossens on the outskirts of the town, a new factory had been opened for the purposes of vehicle construction; a splendid factory, then years ahead of its time, and far removed from the industrial grime of mid-Lancashire. Its glass-roofed sheds covered many acres and were fronted by an ornate façade of polished red brick, which was dominated by a high clock tower, a landmark for miles around the flat plain of the Ribble estuary.

This was the home of the Vulcan Motor and Engineering

*'Auto'-Biography*

Company (Southport) Ltd, a company founded by two brothers, keen motoring pioneers, 'Tom' and 'Joe' Hampson; a company which for a number of years was to enjoy considerable success, until nemesis stepped in and made it just one more lost cause. Vulcan cars and trucks gained a reputation for quality and reliability in the days when performance was not the major selling point; when the longevity of a vehicle was of far greater importance than its ability to achieve fifty miles an hour in so many seconds.

The 1914-18 war, with its consequent War Department contracts for troop carriers and ambulances, brought with it the usual speed-up of techniques in manufacture and assembly, with the result that, when peace time returned the firm was ready with a range of vehicles to offer a transport-hungry country.

As the only manufacturing concern of any size in the district, 'The Vulcan' – as the works came to be known – employed a large proportion of the population, and as a high degree of skill was demanded of any employee, the fact that one worked there gave one a certain cachet in the community.

Lines of demarcation, such as restrict production and exasperate employers today, were unheard of in those days. The primary concern of the trades unions was wages, not 'who does what'. If therefore a good metal turner was also a good fitter, then he could tackle both jobs, and if a draughtsman had the ability to take his designs down to the shop floors, and put them into practice, he was encouraged to do so. Having secured employment at the works, father therefore soon found himself involved, not only with design matters, but with production problems in the machine shops, body shops and toolrooms. Many transmission and suspension ideas which were incorporated into the lorries, 'buses and cars built at Crossens in those early years, were the products of his active and creative mind, and the management, quick to recognize ability and talent, rewarded him with progressive promotion. As the factory's output grew, so his status increased, until he became an executive with responsibilities for sales and service. The name of

*Learning the hard way*

'Ernie' Knowles became as well known throughout the trade as was that of Henry Spurrier, chief of Leyland Motors, a rival concern in the nearby town which the 'Vulcanites' regarded as serious competitors. For these were the days when many firms were struggling for recognition, and the next decade or so would show which should survive. Both the Vulcan and Leyland concerns were equally determined that they should be the ones to come out on top, to dominate their particular sphere.

With father's increased status came greater affluence, and he decided to buy a house in an area more fashionable than Crossens, where mother and he first settled and where Tommy was born. He chose one of the houses which are such a feature of Southport, and which were built during the days of the cotton boom by the Manchester magnates who chose the seaside town as a dormitory, and commuted daily to their city offices by fast steam trains. Today these houses look strangely out of keeping in a town which is busily erecting high blocks of luxury flats and modern estates. Nevertheless they are snapped up by speculators and property developers, and turned into profitable flats.

The house chosen by father was in an area much favoured by his fellow departmental heads, and was well served both by tramway and electric railway for the purpose of commuting to the works. And to mother it seemed that, from the outset, the house became a mere extension of those works for, each evening, father would assemble a group of his colleagues, and, sitting around the kitchen table, they would discuss and thrash out design and production problems far into the night. Whether my arrival on the scene some three years later, alleviated, or merely increased mother's boredom, she was always too tactful to say. I do recall however, that when I reached an age at which I commenced to take an interest in father's work and in things mechanical, there were many sighs of resignation from her direction.

Father delighted in testing personally any new model which was produced at Crossens, whatever its shape, size or purpose, and, although Tommy and I would know that the loud noises

## 'Auto'-Biography

emanating from outside the house signalled his arrival home, we could never recognize by sound just which mode of transport he had selected on any given day. If the noises were sharp and clear, then we would expect to see a car of some description parked in the driveway. If however, they were distant and muffled we would know that, whatever was creating the glorious din would be standing out on the cobbled roadway; that it would be too large to negotiate the gap between the two yellow sandstone pillars, which marked the entrance and tried hard to lend an air of dignity to the house. And seldom was the chosen vehicle the same on two consecutive days. It could have been a two-seater 'doctor's runabout', a four-seater open tourer, a chassis and cab of what would eventually be a lorry, an ambulance or even a twenty-seater char-a-banc. When one day he arrived home at the wheel of a fire-engine, Tommy and I thought we had seen everything, but not a bit of it – the very next day he chose a double-decker bus. On one occasion we felt sure he had come home by train, for his arrival had not been accompanied by a fanfare of noise. Mother was furious when on glancing out of the window she saw that this time he had come home by hearse!

However much the transport varied in outward appearance and in purpose, all shared one feature, for surmounting the brass radiators of each would be a four-inch high mascot, also of brass, and depicting Vulcan, god of fire and metal-working in Roman mythology. Bare of chest, sinewy of muscle, he stood holding in his right hand a hammer, poised to strike at a billet of metal which, held by long pincers in his left hand, rested on an anvil. This was the symbol and trademark of the Vulcan Motor Co, and I loved this statuette, all it stood for, and around which my early years seemed to revolve. That it also served the mundane purpose of being the radiator cap and was unscrewed whenever the water required topping up, I chose to ignore. Any of these mascots found to have imperfections after casting were sent to the carpenters' shop, where they were affixed as decorative handles to desk rocker-blotters, and were issued to customers and 'prospects' for pub-

1. Segrave looks on as the Sunbeam is prepared, Southport March 1926

2. Final adjustments

licity purposes. Of course many were 'acquired' by management and staff, and for many years my father's stood on my own desk, a constant reminder of days long gone. During a removal to another house it was lost, and I would love to have one again.

Perhaps my greatest joy as a youngster was the complete freedom I had to wander around the factory at the weekends and during school holidays. Warned to keep from under people's feet, but to make myself useful if I could, I soon became familiar with all the many processes which went into the making of a Vulcan car or lorry. At first I tended to gravitate towards the offices, where a team of girls sat pounding away all day at a battery of Underwoods, Smiths and Remingtons, on which machines I taught myself the four-fingered school of typing which I still use today. The girls were supervised, theoretically, by 'Lizzie', father's chubby, middle-aged secretary, whose round bespectacled face would peer around his office door with a mock-stern look if the girls chattered or giggled too audibly. A kind soul, she was always ready to conjure up a chunk of toffee or a 'Nuttall's Minto', and always saved foreign stamps for me, cut from the envelopes of incoming mail.

As I grew bolder, and began to explore the factory floors, I became fascinated by the many and varied departments, and I remember to this day the smells of the upholstery shop, where leather was shaped and cut for seating, and the carpenters' shop, where wood was sawn, planed, polished and bent for body frames. I remember too, standing on a wooden box whilst the mysteries of a centre-lathe or a grinding machine were unfolded for me by friendly craftsmen, and watching white-hot metal being poured into sand in the moulding sheds. And I fell for all the tricks which are the lot of any apprentice, such as being sent to the stores for a glass hammer, a box of rubber screws or a bubble for a spirit level.

Father, taking me into the repair shop one morning, asked the foreman to find me something useful to do. This cheerful character, who must nevertheless have possessed a sadistic streak, armed me with a bucket of paraffin and a paint brush, telling me

## 'Auto'-Biography

to clean thoroughly a massive lorry engine which stood in a tin drip-tray on the shop floor. As I flailed the brush between bucket and engine, and as the original grey paint of the engine slowly began to emerge from beneath the grime, most of what I was removing transferred itself to me, with the result that, when I had completed the task to the foreman's satisfaction, I was almost unrecognizable. Pointing to a doorway, one of the workmen told me to go through and clean myself up. I was intrigued to find myself in a whitewashed room, in which there was not only a row of washbasins, but a series of smaller rooms, each without a door, and in each of which sat a man, pipe or cigarette in mouth, and reading a newspaper. When, later that day I asked father for an explanation of what I had seen, he told me that I must have stumbled into a board meeting. I have of course since realised, that I had in fact entered one of the temples which are to be found in any factory, and in which the peculiarly English tribal rite, that of studying the form of horses or football teams, is regularly observed. Nowadays of course doors are added to the cubicles.

By the time I reached the age of eight, not only was I very familiar with the factory and enjoying a friendly relationship with both management and employees – who must have been a tolerant lot – but I had already travelled some thousands of miles, either as passenger with father, or the various works drivers who took out new models for road tests. And these test runs were good fun, as they usually included a visit to what was then a notorious hill-climb, Parbold, some eight miles from the factory. Here, on a gradient which a modern car or commercial vehicle treats with contempt, engines, gear-boxes and differentials would be put to the test, and, as each driver seemed to clench his teeth and adopt a determined expression, I would emulate him, leaning forward as he did, as if by so doing we were urging the vehicle to the summit. And at the summit, whilst the transport was parked to cool off, we would have a cup of steaming tea in a little whitewashed cottage, and here, more often than not, we would find a Leyland lorry parked, its driver also sipping tea inside the cottage. Over an

*Learning the hard way*

exchange of Woodbines, the two men would discuss the rival merits of their respective mounts – an ideal set-up in fact for a spot of industrial espionage.

I suppose I was subconsciously assimilating driving knowledge and techniques whenever I went on these trips, and certainly I came to recognize by the note of the engine, just when a gear change, up or down, was due. I learned many of the tricks of engine and carburettor tuning from the various drivers, as they stopped frequently to effect adjustments, and, as many of them hoisted me on to their laps and allowed me to steer, when I first came to actually drive, the skill was there quite naturally. The transport I chose, however, for my maiden trip, was somewhat unusual.

Father extended his interests in the twenties, to take an active and financial part in the development of another, much smaller firm. This was the British Electric Vehicle Co Ltd, which was turning out electric service trucks in tramsheds abandoned by the Southport Corporation when they changed their tramway system from single to double decked trams. These trucks, forerunners I suppose of the modern fork-lift trucks, were constructed in considerable numbers, and sold to factories and railway companies. And father, taking with him data and brochures went to Paris and succeeded in selling the trucks to the French naval yards. These 'BEVs', as they were called, were used in the Vulcan works for the transport of castings from moulding sheds to machine shops, and of machined parts to the assembly shop, and it was on these that, between the ages of eight and nine I essayed my first solo runs.

The trucks were of simple design and equally simple to operate, being merely four-wheeled platforms, some six feet in length by three feet wide, terminating in a vertical bulkhead, behind which stood the operator. Constructed of heavy solid timber and edged with steel; carrying six batteries in a sling beneath the platform, their overall weight must have been considerable. Two levers projected at right-angles from the bulkhead, its only other embellishment being a meter to register the state of battery charge. The

## 'Auto'-Biography

left-hand lever, when depressed through forty-five degrees, activated an electric motor which powered the rear wheels and gave forward drive, whilst lifting the lever caused the truck to reverse. The right-hand lever was the tiller, also working through a vertical plane, and, via a complicated geometry of linkages, operated on the front wheels. As I once heard a workman telling an apprentice that steering was effected by 'hup for right – dahn for left', this presented no problem to me when the day came that I stepped aboard one of the trucks, and pressed down on the power lever. I had watched carefully on my many visits to the factory, as the operators manipulated them around the shop floors, and thought I knew exactly how to drive them. When, however, I applied pressure to the lever, and nothing happened, I was puzzled. I tried another truck and another, with the same lack of result, so I decided to watch an operator more carefully when the next opportunity presented itself.

I never did spot the trick, for by the time I reached the factory during working hours, the trucks were already spinning around the place, and I finally had to pluck up courage and ask a workman how it was done. Grinning, he pointed to a strip of copper clipped into two prongs beneath the platform, and explained that this fuse was the secret; that without it the truck was immobilized. 'Go on,' he said, 'have a go now!' I stepped aboard and this time, as soon as I depressed the lever, the truck lurched forward, crashing into the legs of a centre-lathe. There were shouts of laughter from the men, but the problem was solved. It was then a simple matter for me to 'acquire' one of the copper strips from the BEV works on one of my visits, and from that time on always to carry my 'ignition key' in my trousers pocket. Eventually I became so proficient as a driver that I was permitted to make myself useful, and to transfer units from one shop to another. Not, however, before I had several mishaps.

The journey from the machine shop to the assembly shop involved the crossing of a covered garage, in which directors' and staff cars were parked during the day. If the huge sliding doors

## Learning the hard way

to the garage were closed, then I could expect a clear, uninterrupted passage between the cars, but if they were open, then I could perhaps expect a car to enter at any time which would present a traffic hazard. A wary eye must be kept open on these occasions and a readiness to avoid a collision. One morning, proudly driving a load of machined castings to the assembly shop, I noticed as I reached the garage, that not only were the doors open, but a car was also entering. With the split second reaction of any good driver I flicked the lower lever up through neutral and into reverse. Unlike a good racing driver, however, I forgot to look behind to see if my road was clear, and of course the inevitable happened. Another truck, following close behind, crashed into mine, and then followed a ridiculous chain reaction 'incident'. The impact precipitated me backwards on to the other truck, and the backs of both my legs were gashed by the leading, sharp edges of whatever it was carrying. Falling to the concrete floor, and observing the blood gushing out, I promptly fainted.

I fully expected to receive a resounding 'rocket' after all this, and perhaps to be banned from driving the trucks again, but, after the wounds had been stitched and I had spent a week or two hobbling around, I found myself being encouraged to resume my role as a reserve driver. Perhaps father and the workmen believed in the theory that if one should fall from a horse, one should remount at once, to maintain one's nerve.

Although there were no L-plates, or driving tests in those days, the legal age at which one could acquire a driving licence was sixteen. When therefore, I reached the age of ten, and became anxious to drive 'properly', the thought of the six interminable years which stretched out before me caused me anguish. Father, however, solved the problem, and I found that I was able to use those years profitably in learning how to handle a car or indeed a heavy commercial vehicle, on the wide, smooth, sandy beaches which are such a feature of the Lancashire coastline, and which stretch from the estuary of the Ribble to that of the Mersey. Here, on summer evenings and at week-ends, he taught me to drive with – I like to

## 'Auto'-Biography

think – some degree of his own skill. Using debris washed up by the tides he would lay out test areas, 'slaloms' and 'garages', much the same as those used today by motor clubs for their competitive driving tests. He had wooden blocks made which clipped on to the clutch, brake and throttle pedals, bringing them closer to my outstretched feet, and, supported by a cushion at my back, I learned to judge distances and to reverse into narrow gaps; how to double-declutch and to assess engine revs in order to effect silent gear-changes with the heavy, slow, 'crash' gear-box. And, during one particularly severe winter, when even the sea froze over in the shallows, the beach was so slippery that father was able to teach me skid control, instructing me how to induce skids and how to steer into them in order to point the car in the required direction once more.

I was not over-indulged by any means. Father never intended me to be just a driver, without knowledge of how to cope with any emergency which may arise – and in those days, emergencies were the rule rather than the exception. I had to learn to grease the many nipples which were fitted to these early vehicles; how to maintain a battery in good condition, and he insisted that I always keep the engine compartment as spotlessly clean as the outside, even to the extent of using 'Brasso' on the copper fuel lines. I had to know exactly where a jack should be positioned beneath a heavy chassis, and how to chock wheels to prevent the vehicle from rolling off the jack on uneven ground. And I had to know how to remove wheels, repair punctures and refit tyres to their rims without damaging either tyres or knuckles. He taught me in fact, motoring in the true sense of the word, and in the repair shop at the works he saw that I was taught how to strip an engine down, to decarbonize, grind valves, set tappets and time ignitions.

The family's favourite car was a Vulcan 12 h.p. four-seater open tourer, a works staff car which seemed to be one of the 'perks' of father's job. I loved this car, and it seems in retrospect that I always associate it with hot summer days, when the canvas hood was folded down, the mica side curtains stowed away, and the leather seats, heated by the sun after standing outside the house, burning the backs of my legs. The car had an extra windscreen for the use of the back seat occupants, which they could raise or lower according to their needs, and on the dashboard – which was of polished wood – next to the speedometer was a Smith's clock, wound up by rotating its knurled brass rim. Mounted on the nearside running board was the battery box and spare wheel and, on the offside, a padlocked toolbox. 'Grey Lady' we called her, and grey she certainly was, this being the colour in which most of the cars and lorries made at Crossens were finished, unless otherwise specified by customers. That she was no lady, she once demonstrated in no uncertain manner.

One summer evening father drove us all down to the beach, and as mother and he decided to sunbathe, I took Tommy for a spin in order to show off my prowess at the wheel. He seemed unimpressed, so I put my foot down a little harder on the throttle pedal. Just as we were travelling at around fifty miles an hour, we ran into a sand gully which is caused by the emergence of a fresh water stream from the sand dunes on its way to the sea. This stream, 'Fine Jane's' as it is called locally, encircles the town of Southport and makes it virtually an island. I had of course forgotten all about the gully, and that it was usually carrying quite a depth of water, and as the car hit it at speed, spray flew in all directions. The car's impetus carried us almost to the opposite side, but, just short of it, the engine stalled, drenched by the water thrown by the wheels. Tommy howled with laughter as, tripping on the running board as I leapt out, I fell flat on my face in what must surely have been the deepest and muddiest part. Maintaining as much dignity as I could, I unhitched the starting handle from its leather 'scabbard' which was suspended by a thong from the 'dumb-iron' of the chassis, and engaged it in its 'dogs'. Carefully moving the handle downwards through half a revolution, I then yanked it upwards sharply. This was usually sufficient to start Grey Lady's engine, providing of course that the manual throttle and ignition controls had been correctly set. I knew that these

## 'Auto'-Biography

controls – levers operating in quadrants in the centre of the steering wheel – should be positioned opposite pencil marks drawn on the quadrants by father for my benefit, and that on no account should I attempt to 'swing' the starting handle before these adjustments had been made. However, in my haste to 'recover face' in front of Tommy, I forgot my drill, as I was soon to realize, for, as the handle reached a point midway in its upwards arc, Grey Lady's ignition – which must have dried out rapidly – kicked back at me. I seemed to fly through the air before I landed once again in the water of the gully, a sharp pain shooting up my arm. My wrist had adopted a queer attitude, my thumb pointing due south and my fingers due north. Tommy struggled to pull me into the back seat and then set off at a fast run to fetch father to the scene.

Reflecting in the hospital later, as a dislocated thumb was re-located in its socket, and a broken wrist re-set and swathed in plaster, it dawned on me that, not only had I slipped up with my starting drill, but I had also committed the cardinal sin of grasping the starting handle like a cricket bat, with thumb on one side and fingers on the other. I had been warned often enough that the thumb should be on the same side as the fingers and that the handle should be cupped, not grasped. I had only myself to blame.

Unfortunately, this minor accident had a major side effect, for it coincided with my sitting the scholarship examinations for entry to the local grammar school, in which I failed dismally. My parents decided that I should become a fee-paying pupil, and I succeeded in passing the entrance examination. Although I pleaded that my inability to pass the first exam was due to my damaged wrist, I found myself very unpopular for some weeks, until it all blew over.

The car figured in another odd incident towards the end of that summer, and I was delighted that no blame could be attributed to me. Father, always very keen on cricket, played as a fairly useful all-rounder for a Southport team in the local league, and one Saturday afternoon he took us all in the car to the neighbouring village of Hesketh Bank, on whose cricket field we could always be sure of a good match. As the game progressed, with Hesketh

*Learning the hard way*

Bank batting, a certain amount of 'needle' crept into it. One of their team, a huge, burly individual, who must surely have been the village blacksmith, positively refused to be routed. Neither our spin or fast bowlers made the slightest impression on this man's wicket, and he was cracking the ball to all points of the compass. Father then tried an over or two of his own medium paced stuff, without effect, until he decided to change his pace in an effort to achieve a surprise. Lengthening his run up to the bowling crease, he unleashed a ball of which even Freddie Trueman would have been proud, and there were loud 'oohs' from around the ground as the ball beat the bat and missed the off-stump by a mere whisker. Once more he sent down a 'sizzler', but this time the batsman was ready. Stepping down the wicket he swiped at the ball before it pitched, caught it with the middle of the bat, and it sped away on a low trajectory. Had father not parked the car where he did, on the edge of the boundary, that ball must surely have reached the next county; as it was, Grey Lady intercepted it, with her windscreen. Shattered glass sprayed out in all directions, and the ball came to rest on the back seat. Honour was satisfied however with the very next ball. Father employed the same fast run up to the wicket, checked at the last few steps, and sent down a 'yorker' which completely foxed the batsman and took his leg stump.

We lost the match, and the drive home was a very draughty one, but father's pipe seemed to be set at a jaunty angle between his teeth.

As that year came to a close, it was signalling the end of my prolonged silly season. I was becoming aware that other cars than Vulcans existed, and beginning to take an interest in motor racing, trials and hill-climbs, father having taken me with him to a few such events in various parts of the country. Just before Christmas, however, Grey Lady was to be involved in a double incident which afforded me much joy, as it permitted me to 'cock a snook' at father after being on the receiving end of a severe wigging from him.

His greatest joy in life, after his job, was choral music. Coming from a musically talented family, he had discovered that the department in which he excelled best, was the wielding of a baton and the leading of a choir. He therefore became choirmaster of the large red-brick edifice in Southport which rejoices, locally, in the name of 'The Jam Church', so called because it had been built through the philanthropy of Sir William Hartley, of bottled preserves fame. It was father's practice to conduct a performance of 'The Messiah' just before Christmas each year, with a choir augmented by choirs from neighbouring churches, and using professional singers as the soloists, singers who came mostly from his old home town of Bolton, where music thrives and where the people seem to sing as well as the Welsh. As Sir William's daughter, Christiana, was this year mayoress of the town, and had promised to grace the performance with her presence, it was of course father's 'big day'.

We were entertaining the contralto of the day at home, and, as we all left for the church in the afternoon in Grey Lady, father carefully instructed me to leave the church when I heard the organ introduction to the Hallelujah Chorus, and to start the engine of the car in readiness for our departure. Tommy and I endured the entire performance successfully by employing our usual tactic, that of coughing loudly in all the wrong places, in order to ensure that Mrs Quinney, sitting in the pew in front of ours, should turn in her seat and proffer us her bag of peppermints. Taking my cue in due course from the organ, I crept outside and walked to the car which was parked at the rear of the church. Starting the engine successfully I then had the bright idea of driving around to the front entrance to save father the trouble. This involved a reversing manœuvre during which I was temporarily absorbed in ensuring that the front wheels did not scar the closely mown lawn which surrounded the church. Being so absorbed I completely failed to notice that the mayoress's chauffeur was also busy with a similar manœuvre at the front of the building. The Vulcan met the Rolls-Royce with a crunch which sent a shudder down my spine, and, as I stepped out to survey the damage, the chauffeur's language was

## Learning the hard way

anything but suitable for a churchyard. Grey Lady was comparatively unscathed, but the chariot of the first lady of the town had a badly crumpled rear near-side wing. The ticking-off I received in front of the entire congregation as they left the church, left me feeling badly crumpled too.

The next phase needs a spot of explanation. Father had been presented with an ebony and silver baton when he conducted a choir in a work which was broadcast over the radio, and he was extremely proud of this, using it on every possible occasion. However, it was heavy, and after wielding it throughout a lengthy performance, his arm began to tire, with the result that periodically its silver tip would strike the edge of his music stand with a loud click. We called this 'hitting the deck' and after each performance he would ask us how many times he had done it. When therefore, we set off home on this particular day, with the prima donna sitting at the front with father, and mother, Tommy and I in the back seat, father called over his shoulder 'How many times did I hit the deck?', I, still sulking and smarting from my ticking-off, called back, 'At least a dozen.'

Father, greatly incensed, turned in his seat to deny this, and momentarily lost his driving concentration. Grey Lady's front wheels, whose track was of exactly the same width as the tramlines which were set into the town's main roads, dropped into a loop-line, constructed so as to permit one tram to pass another. The wheels followed the lines, the steering wheel spun in father's hands, and the near-side front mudgard had a distinct argument with a tree trunk at the edge of the footpath. As the back of father's neck reddened perceptibly, and the prima donna shrieked with laughter, I felt suddenly considerably better.

## CHAPTER TWO

# Sand in the 'blower'

In retrospect, it seems to me that the Southport of my young days was infinitely preferable to the town it has become today, and I cannot honestly say that I view with much sympathy the many changes which the post-war years and the town's elders have wrought or permitted to be wrought in the name of progress. But then, if one is of my generation, I suppose one may say much the same of any town and, after all, a town becomes what its citizens wish it to be.

Southport's crowning glory, the mile-long, tree-lined boulevard which is Lord Street – comparable only with, and in my opinion, much finer than Princes Street, Edinburgh – is still the main feature of the town. The socialites (and would be socialites) still saunter, and perambulate along its wide glass-veranda'd pavements on a Saturday morning, patronize its coffee houses and trade their gossip. Some of the street's many cinemas, and certainly its theatre, have succumbed to the new religion and have become temples of 'Bingoism'; some of its exclusive shops have been transformed into super-markets and chain-store branches. The northern and southern approaches are now marked by tall blocks of 'luxury' flats, and the street itself, surfaced in red tarmac, seems to have become a vast car-park, with such traffic as can still move, doing so warily down the narrow centre artery. If all this means that affluence has spread from the few to the many, then who shall criticize?

The town scored many notable 'firsts' in its history. It once boasted the longest pier; it certainly instigated and retains the largest flower-show in the world, and has the largest man-made sea-water lake in the country – now a mecca for the northern sailing enthusiast. Some of the finest and most challenging golf-links are in or near Southport, and many of the important international competitions are held on them.

## Sand in the 'blower'

But there was one other 'first', which the keen student of motor-racing history should not overlook. The active and progressive racing committee of the Southport Motor Club – a club which thrived between the wars – promoted sand-race meetings in January, in the twenties. Although much credit must go to the British Racing and Sports Car Club for their promotion of motor racing on Boxing Day, they had in fact been anticipated by the Southport Club by just over a quarter of a century. And the sight of the many hundreds of enthusiasts who braved the often icy weather on these wind-swept beaches, to support these meetings, was ample evidence that the Club's enterprise was justified.

Experience in the measuring and laying out of the track, and in crowd control had already been acquired as a result of the summer programme of race meetings which the Club promoted each year, and which achieved much popularity as the years passed. For it must be remembered that there was little in the way of motor sport for those enthusiasts living in northern counties in those days. True, there were a few trials and a few motor-cycle scrambles, but the only real car racing circuit in the country was Brooklands, the then famous venue for the top names in motor racing; now only a mouldering memory at Weybridge.

The Southport circuit was usually two miles in length, being two straights of a mile each, terminating in two hairpin bends, and the very nature of the surface – fine sand, loosely bonded by the ebb and flow of the tides – created its own excitements. For, as a race progressed, this surface became more and more cut up and furrowed, particularly at the two bends where the drift of the cars' wheels churned up the sand,

Organization was good; the spectators being 'contained' behind rope barriers which were at a safe distance from the track. 'Motor Racing is Dangerous' signs abounded, and the same slogan or reminder was printed across the entrance tickets which one purchased at a barrier at the northern end. There was a splendid natural grandstand afforded by the sand-dunes which edge the beaches, and these same dunes were used as a means of entrance to the track by those who did not wish to pay the modest fees charged by the club. The paddocks and the old Vulcan bus which served as the stewards' and timekeepers' office was situated at the southern end, as was the starting line, and most of the circuit races were run in a clockwise direction.

Following a morning of practice, the programme of the day would usually start early after lunch with a series of standing start one mile sprints, along the landward straight. Then would come the serious business of the day – the circuit races, over ten, fifty and one hundred miles. And the entrants for these races were by no means all northerners, for the quality and standard of these meetings began to attract the 'big' names, names such as Raymond Mays, Malcolm Campbell and H. O. D. Segrave, drivers of whom we had read but had not been able to see in action.

When I saw from the advance publicity posters and read in the motoring press, that Segrave was to appear at the club's winter meeting on January 9, 1926, I was quite determined to see him. For Segrave was my particular idol at that time, and, as a new boy at a new school, I had been 'press-ganged' into marking out rugby pitches on the Saturday in the preceding September, when he had achieved three 'firsts' in three events driving a G.P. Sunbeam. I had been bitterly disappointed not to be there, and firmly decided to ignore any plans my housemaster may have for me on the day fixed for the coming meeting. Luckily for me, there was no rugby scheduled for that particular Saturday.

I remember saying to father, on the Friday evening before the meeting, in a manner calculated to achieve a man to man effect, 'We must certainly go tomorrow, come hell or high water,' and his reply, 'If there is high water, old son, there won't be any races.'

Although not a member of the Southport Motor Club, father had many friends who were, and he would therefore have little difficulty in acquiring the 'Official Car' sticker which appeared on Grey Lady's windscreen just before we set off for the beach. As this was to be my last run in the Vulcan before he bought 'something he had his eye on', father, as soon as we ran down on to the

*Sand in the 'blower'*

sands from the Marine Drive, permitted me to take the wheel and to drive down to the Birkdale end of the beach, where the entrance to the course was sited. And driving a car bearing an official sticker gave me much joy, which turned to unholy glee as we passed numbers of my school-mates walking down to the meeting. I had not realized that, not only would the sticker give us unchallenged entry to the course, but it also opened the barrier to the paddock, where father met his friends and I was able to prowl around studying the cars, the drivers and the mechanics.

It was of course a great thrill for me to see Segrave at close quarters, and to bask in the reflected glory of having a father who actually chatted to the great man. I knew, from my avid reading of motoring journals, most of his recent motoring history; knew that in Grand Prix racing, he drove for the Sunbeam-Talbot-Darracq team in company with the Italian counts, Conelli and Masetti. I knew also of Monsieur Louis Coatalen, the master mind behind the Sunbeam Company; the chief instigator of its amalgamation with the French Talbot and Darracq Companies; and the man Segrave had had to satisfy as to his ability before being allowed to drive for the Anglo-French combine. Such was Coatalen's fame in those days, that the very fact of Segrave's being in his team was sufficient evidence of the driver's skill.

As he had, just three months earlier, won the Brooklands 200 Miles Race, driving a Talbot 1½-litre car (although it was called at the time, by some strange permutation, a Darracq) most of the crowd at Southport hoped and expected that he would use this same car on the beach. If then they were disappointed to find that, on this day he would be driving a 2-litre Sunbeam, their disappointment turned to pleasure, as they watched him give a spirited and skilful display of driving, and 'notch up' no less than four wins in four events, two over the mile sprints, and two in the ten mile events. And, although there were many other cars competing, and much spectacular cornering, my chief memory of the day is of the Sunbeam, painted in a brilliant red, streaking along the beach at high speed, trailing a long plume of loose sand.

*'Auto'-Biography*

From a day during which I had the opportunity of examining at close quarters, such cars as Darracqs, Austins, Bugattis, Frazer-Nashes, Amilcars and Vauxhall-Villiers, and had watched them all in action against the Sunbeam, the news which emerged and gave me the greatest excitement, was that Segrave had really come up to Southport to study the beach itself; to look at it as a possible venue for an attempt at the world's land speed record.

Race-winning and record-breaking cars gained, in those days, just as much prestige for their manufacturers and component suppliers as they do today, and Louis Coatalen was very mindful of the publicity value of success. His Sunbeams had not been enjoying a great deal of success in recent Grands Prix, being overshadowed by the rival Alfa Romeos and Delages, and Coatalen shrewdly began to look at the land speed record as an equally effective peg on which to hang his publicity banners, and as being probably less expensive than racing. This is not to suggest that he planned to substitute one for the other, but if, he reasoned, a works-sponsored Sunbeam could wrest the record from the privately owned Sunbeam which held it at that time – that of Malcolm Campbell – then the recent Grand Prix failures could be forgotten. Segrave not only agreed, but volunteered to make the attempt himself.

This attempt was to be made a few weeks later, and I was to be there to watch, but in the meantime the car on which father had said he had his eye arrived outside the house one evening, and gave me a new interest. Not immediately, however, for that particular day turned out to be one of horror for me, and was to give me a salutary reminder that life was by no means all fun and motor-cars.

One of the punishable offences at school, and one which meant a visit to the headmaster's study if committed and discovered, was meeting, outside school hours, any of the girls of the neighbouring high school. This was of course a farcical rule, and would not be tolerated today, but then we looked on it as a challenge to be accepted and possible repercussions as risks to be taken. The rule applied to both schools, and out of it evolved a practice whereby

3. General view at Southport Sands when Major Segrave attempted to break the World Speed Record, March 1926

4. Hush-hush No. 1 driven by Major H. O. D. Segrave, attempting to create a new world record at Southport, March 1926

5. Major H. O. D. Segrave in Hush-Hush No. 1 creating a new world record at Southport, March 1926

6. – '. . . and he's away.'

*Sand in the 'blower*

a group from one would meet a group from the other outside the town's public library after school. Most of my form-mates indulged in this mild form of 'chicken', and as the groups assembled and started to 'chat each other up', one or two from each would keep a watchful eye on the buses as they drew up near the library. If any of the mistresses or masters emerged from these buses there would be a call of 'steps' from the spotter, followed by a crazy scramble up the library steps as we shot into the building and out of sight.

On the day the new car was due to arrive, although I was anxious to get home and to await its arrival, I nevertheless joined my usual group outside the library and, whoever was keeping a look-out that day must have slipped up badly, for before we knew it our maths master, 'Old Johnny' was upon us, staring balefully at each of our faces; memorizing them. We knew then that doom was inevitable; that punishment the following day would be swift and merciless. Almost any of the other masters would have grinned and turned a blind eye, but not Johnny.

The groups disbanded, and together with a few of my pals I went to catch the electric train home, somewhat depressed. The station which served my own district of the town was so designed that the trains departed from it in the same direction from whence they had entered, the drivers and guards walking the length of the platform to exchange cabins, before taking their train to the town's northernmost suburb, Crossens. Although we were pre-occupied this day, and wondering how many strokes of the Head's cane would be applied to our posteriors the following morning, we did notice a man leave our compartment by the wrong door, and step down on to the ballast of the track. If we thought anything of it, no doubt it would be an assumption that he was a railway employee. We left the train and as usual obtained our penny bars of chocolate from the Nestlé's machine, before turning to watch the train depart.

Moving out and quickly gathering speed, it suddenly pulled up with a scream of its steel-shod brakes, and then reversed into the station. There were shouts, and a sudden rush of porters and passengers to the front of the train, where the driver was staggering from his cabin. Not knowing what to expect, we ran with the small crowd. When we did see the cause of the commotion, we reeled back, sickened and horrified. Whoever had left the train by the wrong door had done so quite deliberately, and, during the few seconds taken by the driver and guard to change ends, had stretched himself across the lines in front of the train. The result may be imagined.

And our day of misery was not yet ended. As we climbed the wooden stairs which led to the road outside, silent and avoiding each other's eyes, we heard a noise like that of a car back-firing and emerged from the station to see a huge dray-horse lying in a tangle of broken harness between the shafts of a council dust-cart. Apparently slipping on the greasy cobbled road, it had broken a foreleg and we had just heard a vet put it out of its anguish.

That evening, after I had stammered out a description of my afternoon's experiences, father understood my refusal to go outside and admire his latest acquisition. If I envinced a slight show of interest when he told me that the new car was not a Vulcan after all, I was feeling too low to follow it up, or even to ask what it was. Tomorrow would do.

When, at school the next morning it became known that a few of us had actually witnessed the station tragedy, our stock rose considerably as we were able to relate, at first-hand – and no doubt over-embellished – the grisly details to our morbidly eager listeners. This temporary popularity even sustained those of us who had been involved in the library incident the previous afternoon, through a painful five minutes with the headmaster, as we listened to a short homily on the evil of our ways, and then received six of his best on the seats of our pants.

I was in better form that evening, and eagerly awaited the arrival of the new car. When it did arrive, I hated the thing at first sight. It was a 'Bullnose' Morris Cowley, just six months old.

Mother disliked it, and even Tommy, to whom a car was usually

*Sand in the 'blower'*

only a means of transport, sniffed a little when he saw it. Our combined reactions first amused, then irritated father, and finally made him scratch his head and wonder what on earth had possessed him to buy such a car.

The Bullnose, brainchild of William Morris, had established him firmly on the map during the doldrums of the early twenties, and in fact by 1925 he had sold over 54,000 of them, making Morris Motors Ltd, at that time the country's largest producers. There was no doubt then of the popularity of this car, so well suited to the staid British conservatism, but there is equally no doubt that my family contributed nothing towards this popularity.

At this period I was beginning to acquire an aesthetic – if juvenile – appreciation of good lines in a car, and most of my school books were decorated with doodles of my favourite car radiators. But that bulbous, 'cobby' rounded effort which disgraced the front of the Cowley, and from which the car derived its name, Bullnose, was most certainly not one of these. Nor that wretched canvas hood, which looked as if it had been nailed on as an afterthought.

The car bore little resemblance, quality-wise, to the Vulcan it had superseded, and this no doubt had something to do with the respective fates of the two manufacturers, and perhaps was one of the reasons for the Vulcan being eventually priced out of the market, while the Morris went on to success. Perhaps Vulcan Motors Ltd, could have used a William Morris themselves, to show them how to trim costs, and how to produce in economic quantity.

I never really knew how father had acquired this car, but I have little doubt he bought it from his friend Percy Stephenson, who owned the largest garage in the town at that time, and held the Morris franchise. It had certainly been a demonstration car, and very little mileage was recorded on the mileometer. Father, however, before he finally submitted to family pressure and parted with the car, added a very considerable mileage.

Whatever faults the Cowley may have had in our eyes, its engine was not one of them. Whereas the Vulcan had been 'a bit of a pig' to start, unless the manual controls had been set just so in their quadrants, the Morris started every time, in all conditions, hot or cold, wet or dry, with an easy half turn of the starting handle. This pleasant feature was at least some compensation for the looks of the car itself, and this readiness to start no doubt helped to foster the popularity of the model.

The first Cowleys, produced during the Great War, had been powered by American 'Continental' engines, shipped over by William Morris in considerable quantities. When Continental stopped production, Morris was in something of a quandary, until the Hotchkiss Company of France decided to produce a similar engine in Coventry. And with this engine, which developed something like twenty-six brake horse power, the Bullnose continued unspectacularly but adequately through to the mid-thirties. Father had paid £150 for his car, and I believe I am right in supposing that, had he bought it new, he would have paid just under £200.

Although father kept the car for several months, and used it considerably, although it never caused a moment's anxiety nor gave any trouble whatsoever, we never developed any affection for it, and none of us were sorry to see it go. But its replacement, by a car which was to give us so much pleasure, took place much later that year, and in the meantime the Bullnose was to give us a grandstand view of a bit of British motoring history in the making. For in February the promised visit of Major Henry O'Neal de Hane Segrave took place, and with him came a 4-litre Sunbeam. The object of the visit was to be an attempt on the world flying kilometre and flying mile records, and, as he had promised in January, the venue was to be our own beach at Southport.

The two records were held at the time by Captain Malcolm Campbell. He had purchased from Kenelm Lee 'Bill' Guinness (whose initials gave the name to the KLG sparking plugs) the 350 h.p. Sunbeam which Guinness had been driving with great success at Brooklands. Campbell, after adding a certain amount of streamlining to the car, gained with it, on Pendine Sands in July 1925,

## Sand in the 'blower'

the flying kilometre record at a speed of 150·87 m.p.h. and the flying mile at 150·76 m.p.h.

Segrave arrived at Southport quite early in February, and, together with a few schoolmates, I spent as much time as I possibly could down on the beach, even to the extent of playing hookey from school on more than one occasion. Although he had something of a reputation for being autocratic and somewhat aloof, we came to know him as the friendliest of characters, always ready and willing – even though preoccupied with problems – to answer intelligent questions from schoolboys who were obviously keen to learn. Perhaps there was something of the schoolboy in his own make-up. Certainly in our eyes he looked every inch the man we thought a record breaker should look, as he busied himself around the car, dressed in white racing overalls and wearing a white flying helmet, goggles pushed up on his forehead.

The car itself fascinated us, and gradually, out of conversations with Major Segrave and his engineer Mr Irving, and from reading the motoring press, we came to know the history of this car.

Louis Coatalen was very anxious that when the records were next broken, they should be broken by a Sunbeam car, and that the Sunbeam Company should 'cash in' on the resultant publicity. Knowing then that the 2-litre Sunbeam 'sixes' were much too under-powered and could easily be outpaced by the Delages and Alfas in Grand Prix racing, he decided that these were certainly not record breakers, but from them, and embodying many of their components, he could produce the car to do the job.

He therefore produced a V12 engine, employing two of the 2-litre blocks and mounting them at an angle of 75 degrees on a specially designed crankcase. He then supercharged the engine with a Roots 'blower' and the result was a 4-litre which developed 296 b.h.p.

In looks, the car was not dissimilar to the Grand Prix car, but the length of the bonnet had been increased, beyond the radiator, by a streamlined cowling, at the front of which was a narrow vertical air intake. With the name 'Sunbeam' emblazoned in white paint on the leather-strapped bonnet, the car looked purposeful.

Segrave was so confident in his car, that a decision was reached, that not only would he go for the kilometre and the mile, but an attempt should also be made on the five mile record which was also held by Malcolm Campbell. And to this end trials commenced which were to show that this business of record breaking was by no means easy; that although the car may have the necessary power, and the driver the necessary ability, the choice of surface on which attempts should be made was of paramount importance. For, although the beach at Southport afforded no worries as to length and was consistently flat for many miles, the very nature of its surface – sand, fine and dry after a prolonged period of strong wind – was to cause trouble.

After a trial high speed run one afternoon, Segrave leapt from the car with a worried expression on his face, and when engineer Irving opened the bonnet it was found that the alloy casing of the Roots blower had distorted and cracked. Sand had entered, friction had been set up and heat generated, with devastating results.

Further runs on successive days produced the same results. The car obviously had the potential, but the blower casing failed no less than five times. Segrave, his own facilities for coping with such a problem limited, had no lack of offers of help. The Southport Motor Club and many local garage proprietors tried to assist; father offered the use of the Vulcan repair shop, but none could help with this specialized problem. Irving, in despair, suggested that the project be postponed, and that he should take the car back to the Midlands and there replace the offending supercharger with two smaller units.

However, Segrave, displaying a degree of impatience unusual for him, was anxious to get on with the job. The course had been meticulously marked out, the official timekeepers of the RAC were available, and he decided that he would attempt the kilometre and the one mile, hoping that the blower would stand up for at least

*Sand in the 'blower'*

a few minutes at high speed. The project was then almost a month old, nothing had been achieved and expense was mounting.

The local grape-vine told all interested parties that the attempt would be made on March 16th, and the cold wind which blew in from the sea that day did not prevent many hundreds from turning up to watch. Father parked the Bullnose about half way along the measured mile, and, with the hood down, we stood, leaning on the windscreen to await events.

Soon, the Sunbeam could be seen streaking towards us from the south, and passed us at what seemed, in those days, an incredible speed. As Segrave slowed the car at the northern end of the course, the engine could be heard crackling and 'spitting back' from its exhaust. The return run seemed to be even faster, and there was considerable excitement amongst the onlookers when the car was seen to leave the ground, at a point just opposite our viewpoint, and to become airborne for perhaps fifteen to twenty yards. There was a distinct bump as the wheels struck the sand again, but the car sped on to the end of the course.

We learned the story of those two runs later when we entered the small roped-off paddock. The blower had survived the first run, but on the second, when the car, having struck a small gully, leapt into the air, the engine had momentarily over-revved, being for fractions of a second free from drag, and the blower casing failed again. However, the two runs had been covered at an average speed of 152·33 m.p.h. – just 1·53 m.p.h. faster than Malcolm Campbell's kilometre speed – so that, although he did not achieve his complete target, Segrave gained the world flying kilometre record.

He was not to retain it for long, for, just six weeks later, Parry Thomas, driving his 26·9-litre car 'Babs' on Pendine Sands, increased the lead by a considerable margin, his kilometre speed being 169·29 m.p.h. However, although the Segrave record was short-lived, I had been there to see it, and I continued to follow his career in motor racing, motor-boat racing and record breaking both on land and water, although four years were to pass before I either saw or spoke to him again. Of that meeting, more anon.

## CHAPTER THREE

# The 'Hyper-Leaf'

Parental authority having decreed that I should get my head down in an effort to achieve a certain degree of academic knowledge, motoring memories of 1926, after Segrave's visit and at least until October, are somewhat vague. Certainly I went to all the Southport Motor Club meetings on the beach, and noted, with all the other enthusiasts, that a certain Miss May Cunliffe was building up a considerable reputation for herself as a driver, both on the beach and in other north country events. Women drivers were a rarity in those days and perhaps caused an eyebrow or two to be raised among the established male field. Miss Cunliffe, however, determined not to be 'merely a pretty face', soon began to collect 'pots' and trophies as she demonstrated a skill and verve which many a mere male would have envied. And Miss Cunliffe, two years later, was to figure in an incident which, even as I pen these words today, is still a vivid memory.

I would certainly follow all matters motoring by reading all the magazines devoted to the subject which regularly, on their allotted days, would drop through our letter box – father being a keen subscriber.

But, although I would follow the motor-racing calendar with undiminished interest, most of that year was taken up with school affairs, as I tried to emulate Tommy. He had now left the same school, and left it with an enviable record, gained both scholastically and on the sports field, having played for the first fifteen and first eleven. Little of his glamour was ever to rub off on to me however. Academically I was to be a middle-of-the-roader, usually finishing around the bottom half of my form in maths, science and physics – subjects which 'mattered' in the eyes of my parents –

## The 'Hyper-Leaf'

and around the top in English, French and Art – subjects which did not.

As for the sports field, although I began to regard myself as a useful right wing three quarter at rugby; played for my house and even had visions of playing for the school, I tackled an opponent one afternoon with what I thought was great courage, missed him completely and only succeeded in breaking a collar-bone, after which my interest in the game seemed to wane. At cricket I fared better, having inherited much of father's love for the game. Bowling a 'hat-trick' during an inter-form match one day, I found myself as a result elevated to the house eleven, and then to the school second team.

However, the very average school reports which turned up with depressing regularity at the end of each term, left mother and father with no illusions that they may have produced a genius. Comments written by various masters such as 'He makes rapid forward progress, in all directions', and 'He exhibits great negative potential', were not conducive to inspiring confidence that I should have a brilliant career.

'Never let it be said that he didn't try,' said mother.

'I agree,' said father. 'He's very trying.'

The high spot of that year came towards the end, when I made my first visit to a Motor Show. With his endearing habit of springing pleasant surprises, father dashed home one Friday afternoon, told me to clean myself up and to 'put some decent clothes on'. Almost before I had realized what was happening we were speeding, first by electric train to Liverpool and then by express steam train to London; six of us in the party, father being accompanied by two of his Vulcan colleagues who had also brought their sons along.

And my first Olympia was a memorable one, as I was able to see almost all the cars I had ever heard of, assembled *en masse* in the one great hall. We boys explored the show in a separate group, and amongst the salesmen on the various stands found several who were sufficiently patient to answer our questions. We also found

*'Auto'-Biography*

several who were not, and we gazed with some awe at the 'high priests' on the Rolls-Royce and Bentley stands, who seemed to regard us with disdain. The accessory stands were quite fascinating, for 'bolt on goodies' are by no means products of the postwar years. There were spot-lamps and fog-lamps in profusion, and, until we saw them all displayed none of us had realized just how many 'audible warnings of approach' existed. Bulb horns, electric horns and manually operated klaxons – enough to instrument a Hoffnung orchestra – and all capable of producing satisfactory noises. We knew this, for we tried them all.

As we all met at the end of an extremely interesting day, we boys staggering under loads of brochures and other literature, and went along to Euston for the night train home, all were agreed that the most memorable feature of the show had been the Riley Nine Monaco.

This little car, which proved to be the show stealer, was the first design to bring a new look to the motoring twenties. The windscreen sloped back at a gentle angle, the rear panel and window at a complementary angle, and together disposed once and for all with the 'everything at ninety degrees' attitude which had been the designers' yardstick up to that time. From its nickel-plated radiator of classic Riley contour, to its small luggage 'boot' mounted at the rear, the car had a sporting look, and the longish bonnet, the wire wheels and the swept back front wings all added to this impression.

Although there had been no hint from him, some two months after the show it became obvious that the Monaco had so impressed father, that he decided to buy one. The Riley, in gleaming black, appeared outside the house one day, and the Bullnose vanished from my ken.

Classified, for taxation purposes, as a 9 h.p. the Monaco had an 1100 c.c. engine, of four cylinders with twin high-lift camshafts, and opposed valves in hemispherical combustion chambers. All this I learned from the 'blurb' accompanying the car, and from either a *Motor* or *Autocar* road-test which was published around

## The 'Hyper-Leaf'

that time, I learned that the car might be expected to have a top speed of about 60 m.p.h. And so it proved, for, after a most meticulous running-in period, father took me out with him to the coast road leading from Southport to Hesketh Bank, and there we had the satisfaction of watching the speedometer needle creep up to 63 m.p.h.

This car, with its taut ride, splendid steering and brakes, proved to be full of character. The acceleration and roadholding were good and its thirst for fuel modest. My only complaint was that its arrival seemed to have put a stop to my own driving, for father positively refused to take the Riley down on to the beach, which was still the only 'road' available to me. Although, knowing full well the abrasive qualities of sand I fully appreciated his reasons, I felt deprived and very fed up for several weeks. Oddly enough it took a visit to the famous hill-climb, Shelsley Walsh, to change father's mind and give me the chance of driving again.

Listening to a group of drivers at one of the sand-race meetings that summer, I learned that one or two of them planned to enter the September meeting at Shelsley, and that one of these would be May Cunliffe, whom we were all watching with keen interest as she drove her 3-litre Bentley with considerable success at Southport. Tommy and I therefore 'went to work' on father, to persuade him that we really ought to see a hill-climb; that it would widen our experience. He needed little persuasion, being as keen as we were, and, on Friday September 23, 1927, the three of us set off for Worcestershire in the Riley. I mention the exact date, because surely this was the start of a weekend during which more rain fell on the British Isles than ever before!

As we reached a point somewhere between Droitwich and Worcester, the skies darkened, car lights were switched on, and the first few splashes of rain on the windscreen heralded such a downpour as I have seldom seen since – even living as I do in the Lake District. The single screenwiper proved to be hopelessly inadequate to cope with the solid sheets of water which flung

## 'Auto'-Biography

themselves at the car, and our speed was reduced to a crawl. Tommy, spotting the courtyard of an inn, motioned to father to pull in, and in the inn we stayed, for the night, in the company of several other Shelsley-bound motorists. For the rain continued to come down in perpendicular lances for many hours; the road was awash and nearby streams overflowed their banks.

At six o'clock on the Saturday morning, conditions seemed better and there was an exodus from the inn as we all set off to find the venue of the hill-climb. Had we been alone, Court House Farm, Shelsley Walsh – through whose fields the steep climb winds – would have been most difficult to find. But others of the inn party knew the way and we all travelled in convoy, to find, when we reached the entrance to the farm, that the rain of the previous day had turned the place into a mudbath. The orchard which was allocated to spectators as a car park, the competitors' paddock and the farmyard were quagmires, and we began to wonder if our long journey had been wasted. Although competing cars were arriving at frequent intervals in the paddock and the air became noisy with the crackle of exhausts as engines were 'run up', we felt that conditions were so bad that cancellation of the meeting was inevitable.

We reckoned without the splendid administrative team at Shelsley, however, for, an hour after our arrival we learned that the day's programme was 'on', and, fortified in the knowledge that we had parcels of sandwiches and flasks of hot coffee, supplied by mine host of the inn, we found our way from the orchard to the public enclosure half way up the hill.

This was my first 'Shelsley' – although it was certainly not to be my last – and I had swotted up all the information I could glean about the hill. The timed section of the climb is little more than a thousand yards in length, but it is a very tortuous thousand yards having four major bends and many smaller ones. The start with its timing box is in the farmyard and the hill winds up steeply between thickly wooded areas until it 'breaks' suddenly into open fields at the summit, where the finish line is sited. Competitors'

## The 'Hyper-Leaf'

cars then return to the paddock via a separate road across the fields and down through the woods again. The view from the public enclosure takes in a long, fast straight and two of the major turns, and, although always very crowded is certainly the best spot for 'vision, sound and atmosphere'.

Although, just as the meeting commenced, the skies opened up again and rain lashed the hill, transforming it into a running stream, the crowd had a good day. B. H. Davenport in his Frazer-Nash carved a full second off his own record which then stood at 48·8 seconds, with a most spectacular drive. His extremely light, single-seater, twin-cylinder $1\frac{1}{2}$-litre car, 'Spider', had brought a new challenge to the previous record holder, Raymond Mays, and Mays, on this particular day had to give him best. He drove his white Mercedes, hatless in the downpour, roared up the hill and through the turns in a cacophony of noise, but was slower than Davenport by two-fifths of a second.

We watched May Cunliffe as, with a spirited drive, she achieved a creditable 53·4 seconds in her Bentley, a time which gave her a win in her class, and we also saw once more the twelve-cylinder, 4-litre Sunbeam with which Segrave had gained his record at Southport. This time it was in the hands of W. R. Perkins, whose more usual role was that of racing mechanic to the official Sunbeam team. His time of 55 seconds – fast enough to win him his class – was no mean feat with such a handful of a car on such a narrow road, and showed that he was certainly no novice as a driver.

There were many other exciting exhibitions of driving, and some hair-raising cornering in the appalling conditions. One driver lost both off-side tyres from his wheel-rims, giving the crowd a tense moment or two before he subdued the car. I have to confess however, that the chief memory I carried away from the hill at the end of the day, was of the weather and the mud.

I have before me on my desk, the full results of the meeting at what should perhaps have been renamed Shelsley 'Awash'. It may serve to revive memories for some of my own generation.

45

*'Auto'-Biography*

*Class*

| | | |
|---|---|---|
| Sports up to 750 c.c. | Barnes (Austin) | 63·4 seconds |
| Racing up to 750 c.c. | Caldicott (Austin) | 61·6 seconds |
| Sports 751 c.c. to 1100 c.c. | Churton (Amilcar) | 64·4 seconds |
| Racing 751 c.c. to 1100 c.c. | Mucklow (Frazer-Nash) | 52·2 seconds |
| Sports 1101 c.c. to 1500 c.c. | Newsome (Lea-Francis) | 59·6 seconds |
| Racing 1101 c.c. to 1500 c.c. | Davenport (Frazer-Nash) | 47·8 seconds |
| Sports 1501 c.c. to 2000 c.c. | Fairrie (Bugatti) | 59·8 seconds |
| Racing 1501 c.c. to 2000 c.c. | Mays (Mercedes) | 48·2 seconds |
| Sports 2001 c.c. to 3000 c.c. | Clay (Sunbeam) | 65·8 seconds |
| Racing 2001 c.c. to 3000 c.c. | Cunliffe (Bentley) | 53·4 seconds |
| Sports 3001 c.c. and over | Hall (Vauxhall) | 56·8 seconds |
| Racing 3001 c.c. and over | Perkins (Sunbeam) | 55·0 seconds |

And, as I have stated, this visit to Shelsley regained for me the pleasure of being able to drive on the beach again at home, and I had Shelsley's mud to thank for that. For, as we returned to the orchard car-park and the car, and father tried to drive away, the

## The 'Hyper-Leaf'

Riley's rear-wheels churned themselves deep into the quagmire until the car rested on its toolbox, which was slung beneath the off-side running board.

By dint of much shoving and pulling, and helped by others whose cars were also bogged down, and whose help we reciprocated, finally the Riley became unstuck and we set off for home which we reached in the small hours of the morning, our enthusiasm for motoring having by this time temporarily waned.

Shelsley's weather completely knocked the newness out of the car in father's eyes and after this adventure he had no further qualms about taking it down to the beach and permitting me to resume my driving. Needless to say I took every advantage of this new mood, and I believe the Riley was really the start of an ever growing affection for the products of the firms which now constitute 'British Leyland'. Although future years were to see me either owning or handling cars of most British marques, those which afforded me the greatest pleasure were either Rileys or MGs, certainly the true pre-war productions and even the post-war badge-engineered derivatives.

My joy in driving the Monaco, however, was to be short-lived. Vulcan affairs were not prospering during the years 1927 and 1928 and father and his colleagues were not at all happy about the way things were shaping at Crossens. In 1923, a liaison, or 'arrangement', had been concluded between Vulcan Motors Ltd and Lea-Francis Ltd of Coventry, both concerns hoping that the move would provide the 'open sesame' to a successful future. It was a curious liaison, as I shall attempt to show later, and one destined to snuff out both marques eventually.

The first faint signs of the coming demise of Vulcan Motors, and a drastic change in my family's way of life, were recognizable even to me when father decided to sell the Riley, in order to recover some of the money he had expended on it. As neither Tommy nor I had ever heard any talk of financial problems in the household before, we were concerned and wondered what was afoot. We knew of course that 'the old man' had twice left the Vulcan after

## 'Auto'-Biography

differences of policy had upset him, and had joined friends in other engineering ventures in the town. We knew too that he had returned each time to his first love. When, on his second return, he was given his own new sales and servicing department in the centre of Southport, we had assumed that he would now settle down permanently with an autonomous job and far enough away from warring factions at the main factory. Certainly we were not to know at the time that an almighty crunch was on the way.

When, reluctantly, we said farewell to the Riley as a new owner drove it away, father decided that we would once again use a works car for personal transport and this time chose a Lea-Francis, a car in which, up to that time, I had not taken a great deal of interest. It turned out to be a 1926 open two-seater G-type which, if memory serves me well, was powered by a 10 h.p. 4-cylinder Meadows engine of $1\frac{1}{4}$ litres and with overhead valves. As the criterion by which I judged a car in those days – and indeed to some extent now – was its radiator cowling, I became at once a Lea-Francis addict. For certainly the sculpted cowling appealed to my juvenile taste, and obviously any car which presented to the road such a noble frontage must be a good one. Even Tommy took an immediate interest in this car and, to my intense dismay – he now being old enough to hold a driving licence – was permitted to drive it and so to cut a dash with his friends at the cricket club, for, until one raised the canvas hood and thus completely spoiled its lines, the car looked sporty. My own activities were of course still confined to the beach where, on those long, windswept, sandy reaches I made the most of every opportunity to come my way.

1928 gave me a remarkable chance to watch motor racing in what I still consider to be its best and truest form, when standard production cars – the same cars which could be seen taking father to the golf club or mother to the shops – competed one against the other with the purpose of 'proving the marque' for the benefit of sales. The hugely tyred projectiles, shaped like wedges, which are today seen streaking around the circuits, were then still things

7. May Cunliffe with her father at Southport, 1928

8. Kaye Don in Lea-Francis 'Hyper-Sports' No. 28, eventual winner of the 1928 Ulster Tourist Trophy race

9. The Kaye Don 'Hyper-Sports' Lea-Francis

10. Motor-racing in a blizzard at Birkdale Sands, 1931

## The 'Hyper-Leaf'

to evolve in a distant future. In my young day one could be reasonably sure that one could buy from a showroom the same models of the cars which were being so brilliantly handled by such road-racing stars as Kaye Don, 'Tim' Birkin and Malcolm Campbell. The modern cult of saloon car racing bears some slight resemblance to the early days of racing – the days I knew – although these cars are now 'souped up' to such an extent as to be almost unrecognizable.

One Saturday morning in early spring a knock at our front door heralded the arrival of 'Len' Rhodes, Vulcan's chief tester. He instructed me to don a cap and warm coat and to join him outside. When I did so I found him sitting at the wheel of a car which, to me, looked incredibly beautiful. Today no doubt it would be described as equally incredibly ugly. It was a Lea-Francis to which a sloping radiator gave a new look, and it was a very purposeful-looking car indeed. Wire wheels with knock-off hub caps were surmounted by cycle type mudguards; the bonnet was secured by heavy leather straps and the spare wheel, mounted on the off-side, was similarly secured. In my mind's eye I see the car now, and I can even remember its registration letter and number – WK 6847.

This, Len explained, was a 'Hyper Sports' and it was the car which Kaye Don planned to take over to Northern Ireland and in which he would compete in the forthcoming Ulster Tourist Trophy Race. As I squeezed into the narrow confines of the two-seater cockpit, he told me that the engine was of $1\frac{1}{2}$ litres and was supercharged by a Cozette 'blower'; that the car was capable of speeds around 90 miles per hour and was fitted with vacuum-servo brakes. The petrol tank mounted in the tail would, he said, hold fifty-two gallons and the car was in full racing trim. As we set off for trial runs on the beach and around the town's Marine Drive, I was indeed a proud and no doubt over-cocky youngster that day.

Len drove the 'Hyper-Leaf' at what seemed to me to be fantastic speeds, and demonstrated a skill in gear-changing and double-declutching which I tried hard to emulate in future years. His voice almost drowned in the engine noise and the rush of wind, he managed to convey to me, in reply to my query as to whether it was a Meadows engine, that basically it was, but that the Lea-Francis factory had almost completely rebuilt it. They had fitted, he shouted, low compression heads and pistons, steel connecting-rods and needle-bearing crankshafts. Only the cylinder block and the sump really survived from the original unit.

Although the facts that I had actually been in the car and had travelled at racing speeds, were sufficient in themselves to make this a red-letter day for me, even better things were to come. Father told me that evening that he planned to send me over to Northern Ireland with a party from the factory to watch the TT, and I was overjoyed to such an extent that my enthusiasm had to be quelled, and I was warned in no uncertain terms that if I neglected school-work during the weeks of waiting to cross the Irish Sea, then the trip would be called off. This had a salutary effect, and I put on a show of scholastic effort, inwardly champing at the bit until, at last, the whistle of a railway guard at Southport's station signalled the start of a journey which terminated in the village of Newtownards, in Ulster, and signalled also, for me, the start of high adventure.

The crossing, at night, from Liverpool to Belfast, was memorable for two things. I was one of the very few who were not sea-sick, and I made a friend, whose name I do not know to this day, but whom I was to meet again some two years later when we both witnessed a very dramatic event, which I will describe in another chapter.

As, uneasily, I watched fellow passengers being violently and disgustingly ill, and began to feel decidedly queasy myself, a hand was placed on my shoulder and a friendly voice said:

'Come with me to the sharp end, young feller – you'll be happier there.'

I turned and followed a young man, attired in tweed cap and tweed plus-fours, with a wisp of fair moustache and wearing the

## The 'Hyper-Leaf'

first pair of heavy horn-rimmed spectacles I had ever seen. I hope he reads this, recognizes himself over this long span of years and makes himself known to me. For he proved to be a veritable fund of motor-racing information and, I feel sure, must have been a press reporter or motoring correspondent.

As we stood in the bows, which were illuminated only by the glow of a mast-head light, and attuned ourselves to the fairly violent pitch of the ship, he told me of the race we were going to watch, and 'filled me in' with details of the circuit, the drivers and the rules by which they had to abide. I learned that the Newtownards circuit was thirteen and some two-thirds miles in length, shaped roughly like a school-boy's kite, and had three corners named after the villages through which they passed, Newtownards, Comber and Dundonald. It was a true road circuit which normally carried day to day traffic and its total lap length was such that thirty laps had to be completed to give a race length of 410 miles. Handicapping of the various classes of car was effected by crediting laps, the number varying according to the engine capacities. Thus, for example, 3000 c.c. cars would start from scratch and such cars as the diminutive Austins with their 747 c.c. engines would be credited with five laps. Only standard production cars were eligible and they must have been announced as being available to the public by February. Sales figures had to be shown to the race organizers to prove the commercial purpose of the cars and only fuel which was freely available at road-side pumps may be used. In short, this was a race to fully test the marques and to the makers of the winning cars would go the spoils of victory, in the form of publicity and sales.

I thoroughly enjoyed that night crossing with my knowledgeable and very likeable companion. I learned more from him of motor racing and the contemporary drivers of the day in those few short hours, than I ever learned from my avid reading of the motoring press, and, as I lost sight of him in the rush of disembarkation and rejoined my party, I looked forward to the coming race with even greater eagerness. My enthusiasm for motor racing, undiminished

## 'Auto'-Biography

even today, had its real genesis, I feel sure, in that meeting with a stranger on board a ship.

Details of how the Vulcan party reached Newtownards village, and took up strategic viewing positions behind heavy wooden barricades, are now only vague memories. I do remember listening to the gossip which prevailed amongst the crowd as we waited for the start of the race, and hearing about the withdrawal of the official Bentley and Mercedes teams, the first because of a disagreement over the system of handicapping and the second because of an argument as to how many spare wheels may be carried. I heard too of how, during practice on the previous day, C. S. Bell, entering a corner in his Riley at some 80 miles an hour, slid into a hedge, overturned his car and was flung out, unhurt, into a field. And I certainly remember the race itself.

I watched Malcolm Campbell in a Bugatti, Kaye Don in 'our' Lea-Francis, 'Tim' Birkin in his Bentley, 'Scrap' Thistlethwaite in a white Mercedes and Lord Curzon in a Bugatti – all great names of their day, and all demonstrating incredible skills as they threw their cars into tremendous 'drifts' around the corner which bisected the village, the thunder of their exhausts echoing back from the buildings. And as the race progressed, news filtered through to us that Campbell, slowing to approach the pits after the first few laps, had leapt out of his car as it burst into flame, and had stood aghast as he watched it disintegrate in a huge pall of black smoke. He had been leading the pack with Birkin close behind, and this disaster put Birkin out in front, a position he held for some laps until a broken oil-feed delayed him and allowed smaller cars, with handicap advantages, to take the leading places.

Excitement grew in our small party as it began to dawn on us that Kaye Don was now fighting a personal duel with Leon Cushman, who was driving an Alvis. First the 'Leaf' would enter our corner in the lead and on the next lap, the Alvis. Both had three lap handicaps, and as lap succeeded lap only seconds separated them. On the twenty-sixth lap, Cushman, chasing Don hard, skidded badly as he approached our viewpoint and the gap between

## The 'Hyper-Leaf'

the two cars widened considerably as Don streaked away out of the village. Cushman, however, began to close again as they entered the final lap, and I heard later that only thirteen seconds separated the two cars as Kaye Don brought 'our' car – WK 6847 – past the chequered flag to win, in a time of 5 hours 58 minutes and 13 seconds.

So the car in which I had so proudly sat, and in which I had travelled at over 80 miles an hour just a few short weeks ago; the car we had really come to see, and in which we felt we had a personal interest, actually won the race, against an entry in its own class, of twelve cars – to say nothing of its having 'seen off' the glamorous Bentleys, Bugattis and Mercedes.

As we sailed for home that night, and I – too tired out to worry about such things as sea-sickness – settled down to sleep on a bench in the ship's saloon, I remember that my last naïve thoughts before I fell asleep were that now, after this glorious victory, there need be no further problems for the Vulcan–Lea-Francis people. All would now be well. Naïve indeed.

CHAPTER FOUR

# A lap or two with Billy

If I had been thrilled by the displays of skilful driving I had seen at Newtownards, displays which had firmly established motor racing in my eyes as the premier sport, I was not to be permitted to forget the fact that such a sport is exceedingly dangerous. Indeed I was to be given ample evidence of this when, later that year, on Saturday June 23rd I went down to the beach with my school pal 'Rollo' Benson to watch another sand-race meeting promoted by the Southport Motor Club. The day promised excitement, for to the usual list of northern and midland entries had been added the names of Malcolm Campbell and Raymond Mays, the one fresh from Daytona Beach with the world land speed record to his credit, and the other, the current Shelsley Walsh hill-climb champion.

Although Campbell had a world-wide reputation as being one of the 'greats' of motor racing, the northern enthusiasts who flocked in large numbers to watch this particular meeting, were not at all sure that on his earlier visits to Southport, he had completely mastered the technique of driving and cornering on loose sand. We felt that drivers of the calibre of Jack Dunfee, May Cunliffe, Percy Stephenson and C. J. P. Dobson – regular entrants at all the beach meetings – could perhaps show this southern 'maestro' a thing or two. For driving on sand calls for a considerably different technique to that of driving on tarmac or concrete, especially in the matter of cornering. A driver accustomed to inducing deliberate 'drifts' in order to negotiate a hard surfaced corner in the least possible time and at the highest possible speed, finds his car responding in a most peculiar manner when he attempts to perform the same manœuvre on sand, especially after

## A lap or two with Billy

that sand has been churned up by preceding cars. At times a contrived drift is successfully accomplished, at others it is not, and it is not unusual for a driver – although he feels that he has made a copy-book turn – to find his car pointing back in the direction from whence it came. Thus a hazard can be presented to following drivers who have to execute feats of avoidance, sometimes hilarious, sometimes dramatic. And there is the other possibility, that of the sand bunching up at the sides of the wheels as they attempt to slide, bunching up until the car, the slide completely baulked, overturns.

So we all felt somewhat 'snide' that day and very unkindly and inhospitably hoped that Malcolm Campbell would be 'seen off' by one of our local drivers.

Rollo and I reported our arrival to the officials who sat in the old Vulcan 'bus which served as Race Control, for, thanks to my father, we had several friends among them who slipped us marshals' armlets and told us to make ourselves useful around the circuit. Having performed several small duties around the 're-plenishment' pits as they were then called, and having watched the mile sprints and the ten mile race from that view-point, we crossed the track to the centre 'island' and made our way to the northern corner to await the start of the main event of the programme, the 100 mile race.

The course consisted of a straight mile length on the landward side, on which the starting and finishing points were sited and which led into a wide sweeping corner at the southern end. The cars then returned down the seaward reach, half way down which was an 's'-shaped chicane, and had to negotiate an acute hair-pin bend at the northern end. The 100 mile event would call for no less than 150 corners and it was noticeable that most of the crowd had begun to assemble in the vicinity of these corners.

The premier award for the outright winner was the *Daily Dispatch* 100 guineas gold vase and there were cups for the winners of the various classes, which were 750 c.c., 1100 c.c., 1500 c.c., 2000 c.c., and unlimited capacity. I have before me the complete

*'Auto'-Biography*

list of the thirty entrants who lined up to be escorted around the track on a courtesy lap before the start of what turned out to be a very dramatic race. To any of the sixty thousand spectators who were there, and who may read these words, perhaps the list will revive memories.

| Driver | Car | Capacity |
|---|---|---|
| R. G. Davies | Darracq | 1598 c.c. |
| H. F. Clay | Mercedes | 6800 c.c. |
| F. E. Roberts | Bugatti | 1496 c.c. |
| M. Campbell | Delage | 1486 c.c. |
| G. L. Jones | Bugatti | 1496 c.c. |
| J. F. Field | Bugatti | 1496 c.c. |
| H. Mason | Austro-Daimler | 2994 c.c. |
| I. W. Croft | Austin | 743 c.c. |
| J. Dunfee | Sunbeam | 1988 c.c. |
| M. Sutcliffe | MG | 1802 c.c. |
| D. G. Bird | Amilcar | 1074 c.c. |
| D. Higgin | Talbot | 1500 c.c. |
| R. Mellor | Frazer-Nash | 1496 c.c. |
| A. S. Llewellyn | Amilcar | 1096 c.c. |
| R. A. Bathgate | Bugatti | 2000 c.c. |
| W. H. Hylton | Vauxhall | 4526 c.c. |
| C. Shorrock | Toreador | 1980 c.c. |
| J. W. Jackson | Sunbeam | 2920 c.c. |
| P. Stables | Bugatti | 1996 c.c. |
| R. L. Aspden | Vauxhall | 4480 c.c. |
| C. J. P. Dodson | Alvis | 1496 c.c. |
| C. Bradshaw jun. | Amilcar | 1078 c.c. |
| A. P. Glenny | Frazer-Nash | 1498 c.c. |
| H. A. Smythe | Amilcar | 1047 c.c. |
| P. Stephenson | Austin | 750 c.c. |
| May Cunliffe | Sunbeam | 1988 c.c. |
| A. Drew | Vauxhall | 4526 c.c. |

*A lap or two with Billy*

| Driver | Car | Capacity |
|---|---|---|
| F. B. Taylor | Bugatti | 1990 c.c. |
| R. Mays | Bugatti | 1998 c.c. |
| R. Mays | Vauxhall | 2996 c.c. |
| G. J. Jackson | Sunbeam | 2973 c.c. |

As the cars roared away at the drop of the starter's flag, we noticed that May Cunliffe's car, a 1988 c.c. Sunbeam which had formerly been owned by Segrave, had apparently stalled on the 'grid' and the field had already reached the far, wide turn before she managed to get away in pursuit. From our viewpoint the cars, returning down the angled seaward stretch, seemed to leap straight towards us as they left the chicane, before they slid, bucked and bounced around the hairpin near which we stood. Sand flew in all directions and the corner, which had been raked smooth after the ten mile race, became churned up again and made cornering progressively more difficult. Just how difficult was proved in no uncertain manner when a Liverpool driver, R. A. Bathgate overturned his 2000 c.c. Bugatti in front of us on only his fourth or fifth lap. He sustained a fractured elbow, his mechanic was slightly hurt and the Bugatti showed convincing evidence of the hardness of sand when struck at high speed.

The race progressed and we watched May Cunliffe, after her delayed start, begin to work her way through the field until, at about the half-way stage, she was holding third place. On her thirty-third lap, after a distance of sixty-six miles she made a bid for second place, closing rapidly on an Austro-Daimler 2994 c.c. driven by H. Mason, who was chasing Raymond Mays' 2996 c.c. Villiers-Vauxhall for the lead. As the three cars came up to the hair-pin – each driver noticeably using a different line of approach – Mays and Mason spectacularly but safely negotiated the turn and sped away along the straight in a rising crescendo of sound and leaving behind them that wonderful smell of burnt Castrol. May Cunliffe took a wider sweep than the others in her approach and entered the corner at an unusual angle. Just at the

*'Auto'-Biography*

apex of the hair-pin the Sunbeam juddered rapidly sideways, the off-side wheels left the sand and the car rolled over, to slide upside down for some yards.

Marshals ran on to the track to flag oncoming cars clear of the hazard, and I joined a party which ran to the car. There were cries of 'watch for fire' as we struggled to roll the car over, and in my efforts to help I trod in what seemed to be a pool of oil which was slowly spreading on the sand. When my white tennis shoes turned red I realized that this was blood. As the car bounced down on to its wheels again we saw that May Cunliffe was still at the wheel, but her riding mechanic slumped limply to the sand. It was her sixty-one-year-old father and, a neck artery severed, he died there almost instantly.

We were all sickened at this tragedy, the first grave incident to occur during a Southport Motor Club meeting, and, although the race continued, one or two drivers dropped out as a mark of respect, amongst them Malcolm Campbell.

There was of course the usual controversy as to whether the race should have been stopped; comments about those who retired and comments about those who continued. This controversy seems to have resolved itself today, and a race continues in spite of fatalities, but on that particular day in 1928 much argument raged.

Raymond Mays in his Villiers-Vauxhall Special won the race and the gold vase, Paul Stables in his Bugatti was second and H. Mason with his Austro-Daimler took third place. Of the remaining cups Southport driver Percy Stephenson in his ubiquitous Austin 750 c.c. collected no less than three.

May Cunliffe herself suffered only minor injury and had what could only be described as a miraculous escape. As for the Sunbeam, apart from a bent steering wheel and a dented radiator cowling, it was undamaged.

This was the first death I had witnessed in high-speed events, but, as I shall attempt to show, it was not to be my last.

As the summer of 1928 wore on there were no signs of improvement in the affairs of Vulcan Motors Ltd. A cloud of depression

*A lap or two with Billy*

settled over the town as the large proportion of residents which earned its living at Crossens realized the possibility that the works might close. The fact that disaster loomed over a fairly near horizon even filtered through to me, and I have little doubt that my reactions would be selfish, for it would mean there would be no more casual visits to the works, no more access to unusual cars, no more runs in prototypes and no more contact with the many friendly people it had been my good fortune to meet in my young years.

There were hopes that the firm in the nearby town which was making such successful headway in the commercial vehicle field, Leyland Motors, would step in and save 'The Vulcan'. The Crossens factory had been specifically planned for vehicle production; the skilled labour and the know-how were available, and road and rail access was good. In fact the whole set-up seemed ripe for take-over. I believe that overtures were made and many discussions took place in the board-rooms of both firms, but to no avail, and activities at Crossens came to an end.

Looking back in retrospect and with hindsight, I suppose the firm really had a chequered career. A brief association with Harper-Bean during 1919–20 did little good to finances. There had been experiments with such oddities as a worm-drive V-8 tourer of $3\frac{1}{2}$ litres, two models in 1922 with sleeve-valve engines, a 3·2-litre sports-touring Four and a 1·4-litre, 10 h.p. flat-twin. None of these reached the public and vast sums of money must have been wasted on these abortive designs. Vulcan trucks, 'buses and lorries were good and sold well, both at home and abroad, but their success was insufficient to stave off the eventual demise of the firm which made them.

The liaison effected by C. P. Wardman, Vulcan's managing director, with Lea-Francis, a move intended to be a shot in the arm for both concerns, proved to be good for neither. But perhaps the attempts which were made to find a formula for success are worth remembering.

Vulcan and Lea-Francis pooled their dealer-network throughout the country, and Vulcan undertook to make certain 'Leaf' bodies

## 'Auto'-Biography

and power units, while Lea-Francis produced gear and steering boxes for Vulcan. Vulcan cars began to bear a remarkable resemblance to Lea-Francis and vice-versa. There were several permutations between the years 1925 and 1928 and I suppose one may say that 'badge engineering' came to Southport. At one time the only obvious difference between the two stable-mates was that the Vulcan wore artillery type wheels and the Lea-Francis wire.

In 1928 car production ceased and although commercial vehicles were still in production, they were no longer made in Southport; what remained of the Vulcan business being amalgamated with the firm of Tilling-Stevens. Father finding himself, until 1930, deeply involved in the 'migration' from Southport to – eventually – Maidstone, was invited to join this new amalgamation in an advisory capacity. However, although the terms of the offer were apparently generous, he knew that acceptance would mean leaving Southport, his choir, his cricket club and all his many friends. This he was not prepared to do, and his decision had the complete support of the family, although I knew that his refusal to accept the job was only made after much heart-searching and with a degree of uneasiness. Never a ruthless, 'ambition is everything' type he would, as things transpired, have soon found himself out of his depth. For Tilling-Stevens and Vulcan became absorbed by the rapidly expanding Rootes Group, which had its beginnings in Kent, and the name of Vulcan vanished into the limbo of motoring's lost causes. The god of fire and metal-working finally laid down his hammer.

With many vicissitudes, the name of Lea-Francis survived until 1960. Bankruptcy in 1934–35; reflotation in 1937; cars built until about 1953; disappearance, followed by a brief re-emergence with the abortive 'Leaf-Lynx' of 1960. After this – silence. There have been whispers of revival, so perhaps we may yet see a 'Hyper-Leaf' in contemporary shape jostling with the MGBs, the 'Jags' and the Rapiers, for a place on our claustrophobic road system.

My own young way of life was curiously undisturbed by father's problems. Perhaps by way of a 'perk' from an appreciative board

## A lap or two with Billy

of directors, he managed to retain the two-seater Lea-Francis, and I still enjoyed my week-end driving on the beach. There were also several illicit spins around the quiet roads near home and along the country lanes outside the town. The outcome of course was that I developed a proprietorial feeling about the car, and whenever Tommy borrowed it to go to the cricket club or to take out one of his girl friends, I was intensely annoyed. On his return I would make a great show of re-tuning it, complaining bitterly that it never ran as well after he had been driving it.

Each successive sand-race meeting promoted by the local club attracted larger and larger crowds, and I believe I missed none of these meetings. By this time I had many friends among the drivers and mechanics, and to be recognised by such people as Malcolm Campbell and his mechanic, Leo Villa, and to perhaps receive a nod or even a word from them, would make my day. I even scrounged a ride with some of the drivers as they tested their cars prior to a race. One such ride which was to take place some few years later, in the early thirties was brought vividly back to mind as I read, on the day I penned these words, of the death of an old friend. I will jump forward those few years, to describe the incident.

A driver whom I had been watching with great interest was Billy Cotton, leader at the time of the resident dance orchestra at the town's Palais de Danse, and who was living at a 'select private hotel' owned by a favourite aunt of mine near the seafront. Billy, seeming to fill and indeed to overflow the narrow confines of his cockpits, and with steering wheel well tucked in to his chest, gave stirring exhibitions of sand driving and with no little success.

During one Saturday morning practice session I was watching his car being wheeled from the pit area to the track, when a heavy hand fell on my shoulder, and, turning, I found the hefty be-spectacled band-leader at my side.

'Like a spin young Knowles?'
'Er . . . d'you mean . . .?'
'Yep . . . hop in!'

## 'Auto'-Biography

For the life of me I cannot recall what car that was. Possibly a Riley or an MG, but I do remember that, for five hair-raising laps of the Southport beach circuit, Billy Cotton gave me the finest experience of my life as, his sheer bulk almost squeezing me out of the cockpit, he demonstrated driving techniques which I have tried to emulate ever since. We hurtled down the straights with the speedometer needle wavering satisfactorily between 90 and 100 m.p.h., and when approaching a corner his gear-change into a 'lower cog' was a joy to watch. Clutch depressed, gear lever already moving through neutral, throttle 'blipped', clutch depressed again, and into lower gear – all in one easy movement – and Billy still had time, or an extra hand, to stab a finger vigorously at the grab handle on my side of the dash indicating that I should hang on. I would feel the car judder as it tried to slide on the loose sand, and I knew that the offside wheels were parting company with the sand in several of the corners, before the car would steady and we streaked away down the straight again, Billy wearing a broad grin. Should another car pass us, Billy would indicate his disgust with a Churchillian two-fingered gesture, in reverse, to which the other driver would respond in similar fashion. Should anyone suppose, therefore, that this gesture is a post-war American import, I can assure them that it is as pre-war British as Billy Cotton himself.

Quite soon after this meeting the Cotton Band left the 'Palais' at Southport, and Billy his lodging at my aunt's house. The next time I was to meet him was in the late forties when I found him enjoying a between-acts breath of air, outside the stage door of the Alhambra Theatre in Bradford. I made myself known to him again and we briefly reminisced of the Southport days, before he took me backstage, gave me a drink in his dressing-room and then found me a spot in the wings from which I watched the rest of the show.

Now I learn, some thirty odd years after he allowed me to be his temporary riding mechanic, that, just before his seventieth birthday, he has died. With thousands of others, I am saddened to

## A lap or two with Billy

know that this generous, larger than life character is no longer with us. Equally at home driving at high speed around the circuits at Brooklands, Donington Park or Southport, or conducting his band on the stages or in the television studios of the world – his raucous 'Wakey-wakey!' either infuriating or delighting his listeners – Billy Cotton was a man I was proud to know.

I will now step back again to take up my theme at the point where suddenly, after months of swotting, cricket, girl friends and above all motoring, it was 1930, a year which saw my family's way of life remarkably changed, and in which I was an eye witness of an historical event in the world of speed.

## CHAPTER FIVE

# 'Miss England II'

Fate at times has a damned strange way of steering us in certain directions, and 1930 afforded me an example of this. If I wrote quite simply, that because I took my training for the school sports day seriously, I was as a result led to being an eye-witness of a death on Windermere, I should not be believed. But that is exactly what occurred and to explain it, I must elaborate.

Having, on previous sports days, enjoyed some degree of success as a 100 and 220 yard sprinter, I decided that perhaps hurdling was also within my capabilities, and after asking my housemaster to enter my name for this event I began to train hard both at school on the playing fields, and at home in the back garden. And this business of training at home presented its problems, for the garden afforded only a short running area and no hurdle. There was, however, a brick wall separating our land from that of our neighbour; a wall of just about the right height. I therefore devised a system whereby I would watch carefully and note whenever the neighbours left their house, and then, using a flower bed as a launching pad, I would sprint across our lawn, execute a swift avoiding action around a rose-bush, and leap over the wall, to land softly in a compost heap on the other side. As my running shoes and shorts became progressively dirtier and smellier, so my hurdling technique improved, until I felt I could take on all comers.

One Saturday morning in May, I was either wool-gathering or I lost my correct pace around the rose-bush, for instead of clearing the wall with my newly acquired skill, I struck it with my leading foot and crashed down on to the peaked topping bricks surmounting the wall. They struck me immediately below the ribs, com-

11. Neck-and-neck start in the one-mile race for under 2000 cc: Jack Field in the Talbot, No. 1 and D. Ferranti in the Austin

12. D. L. de Ferranti in the Austin No. 51 and W. L. Thompson in the Triumph No. 39 at Southport Beach, February 1931

## 'Miss England II'

pletely winded me, and I passed out. Then commenced the chain reaction which led me, ultimately, to Windermere. I was carried indoors, placed on a settee and as – tended by my unflappable 'mum' – I came out of the faint, I felt sick. Staggering to the kitchen sink I duly performed and then, passing out again I crashed backwards, my head meeting the protruding knob of the gas-cooker door. This presented a problem beyond mother's skill, for a bump appeared on the back of my head which she later described as a miniature of the Matterhorn. The thing which worried me when I came to my senses again was the fact that I could no longer see, everything being blurred and out of focus. The doctor for whom mother sent explained to her that I had obviously 'shaken' the optic nerves at the back of the skull and that, as I had also cracked a lower rib, recovery may take some time.

My sight returned in three or four days, but as I was still somewhat groggy, father decided that I should spend a few days with friends who had a bungalow near the lake at Windermere. This suited me admirably for, not only did it mean a renewal of a friendship with 'Bertie' Borwick, whose family ran the boatyards at Bowness – a friendship dating from the time father first started to take us all to the Lakes for summer holidays – but news was abroad that Sir Henry de Hane Segrave was taking his speedboat 'Miss England II' to Windermere, his stated purpose being an attempt on the world water speed record. This record was held at the time by the American, Gar Wood, whose craft 'Miss America VII' had given him a speed of 92·863 in September 1928, and, if Segrave intended to take this record from him, then I certainly intended to watch; it would be adequate compensation for a cracked rib.

Segrave at that time had a very impressive history of speed behind him. In addition to his race circuit successes he held three world land speed records, one of which in 1926, I had been able to see him gain on Southport beach. Briefly these records were: at Southport driving a 4-litre V12 Sunbeam he gained the 1

*'Auto'-Biography*

kilometre record at 152·33 m.p.h.; at Daytona in 1927, driving a 44·8-litre twin-engined '1000 h.p.' Sunbeam he gained the 1 kilometre record at 202·98 m.p.h., the 1 mile at 203·79 and the 5 miles at 202·67. Again at Daytona in 1929, this time driving a 23-litre Irving Napier called 'Golden Arrow' he gained the 1 kilometre at 231·44 m.p.h. and the 1 mile at 231·21 m.p.h.

Turning to water in 1927 in order to widen his experience he won races in a variety of craft at such venues as Hythe, the Thames, Miami, Templiner See and the Venice Lido. And, driving one of these boats – the first 'Miss England' – which was powered by a single 930 h.p. Napier Lion engine, he unofficially broke Gar Wood's record at a speed of 93·5 m.p.h. at the Venice Lido. If then, he reasoned, a British boat of 930 h.p. could give him equal speeds to those gained by Wood in a 2600 h.p. boat, then a boat of greater power must easily gain the record for Britain. Thus Miss England II, the boat I was to see launched on Windermere, came to be created. Perhaps, before describing the launching and subsequent fate of Miss England II, this would be the right spot to describe her technically.

There was little above the water line of the new hull to suggest that she was unorthodox. Her three-seater cockpit sited well back towards the stern, her long rakish decking reached forward to terminate in pointed bows, and her stern was V-shaped, a shape intended to minimize drag. She was 38 feet 6 inches in length and her beam was 10 feet 6 inches; her laden weight being $4\frac{1}{4}$ tons. It was in her 'power-house' and her under-water features that Miss England II differed from other craft. For two supercharged 12-cylinder Rolls-Royce engines were installed – aero-engines similar to those used in the Supermarine seaplane which was flown in the Schneider Trophy Air Race. Each engine developed power around 1850 h.p., yet they were intended to drive only one stainless steel two-bladed propeller a mere 13 inches in diameter. Segrave and his fellow designers had attracted much criticism from marine engineers when it became known that the propeller

## 'Miss England II'

of his first Miss England would turn at 6800 revs per minute. Yet the propeller of this second boat was so geared to the power output from the two engines that it would turn at the remarkable rate of 12,500 revs.

As on the first Miss England, there were two rudders on the new boat, one positioned at the bow and the other aft. Beneath the hull was a single planing step or 'wedge', so designed that it was adjustable and permitted experimentation. And it was this step, and its mounting to the hull, which was for many years to be the subject of controversy, and indeed, heated argument amongst the knowledgeable boat-builders of Windermere.

There were no less than twenty-four instruments mounted on the facia-board in the cockpit, and as the engines required two throttles and two clutches, Segrave needed the services of two riding-mechanics who sat on each side of him.

'I don't care to beat the record by a fraction,' said Segrave. 'I propose to make a clean sweep by 20 m.p.h. or so.' This meant that he was expecting Miss England II to have a speed potential of 115 to 120 m.p.h. – no mean ambition in those days of the thirties. And the news aroused keen interest which was reflected by the huge crowds of spectators which collected around the banks of the lake on Thursday June 5th, for this was the day chosen for launching by Lord Wakefield – who had put up the £25,000 which the boat had cost.

As a friend of Bertie Borwick, I was always granted free rein to wander around the numerous wooden jetties and piers at the boatyards, and was therefore able to be 'in amongst it all' when a bottle of champagne was cracked on the razor-edged bow of the boat, and I watched her slide easily and unhurriedly down the slip and into the water – water which was bustling with innumerable craft of all shapes, sizes and motive power. With his two mechanics, Michael Wilcocks and Vic Halliwell seated on either side of him, Segrave started up the engines. A puff of white steam-like smoke was followed by the satisfactory roar of perfectly tuned machinery, before the engines settled to a quiet hum. All very

## 'Auto'-Biography

impressive and everything smacking of the indefinable something which was British 'between the wars' quality.

I watched Segrave as he carefully manœuvred his craft between the many others, and motored it across to Belle Isle. However, instead of opening up the revs and streaking away down the lake, he apparently switched everything off and seemed to be consulting with his team. Within minutes a launch had left the jetty on which I stood, had crossed the intervening water, hitched a rope to Miss England and had towed her back to the slip-way. I then learned that, due to the slow speed at which she had been taken across the bay, water had failed to enter her collection scoops in sufficient quantity, and the port engine had badly overheated. In later years, at another venue and with another contender, I was to see this sort of problem again and again.

It was a measure of the splendid character and complete unflappability of Sir Henry Segrave, that, although he was always so very busy around his boat and in the workshops, he never frowned at my perhaps over-enthusiastic and certainly somewhat juvenile questions during those next few days. He found time to answer them all, and even joked about that 'wretched bit of sand at Southport', when I told him where I had last met him.

During the early evening of June 10th, Segrave decided to give the boat her first fast run, and this time, after ensuring that his course was clear of other craft, he left the jetty at a speed which would ensure that the collection scoops beneath the hull would fulfil their function and give the engines sufficient water to keep them at the correct temperature. With her wake spewing out behind in an ever increasing fan, Miss England streaked away from the northern tip of Belle Isle and planed her way along the measured mile. The first run was effected at what was described as 'above record speed' and, turning, Segrave brought her back. The actual words of Michael Wilcocks, one of the two riding mechanics, as recorded in Cyril Posthumos's splendid book *Sir Henry Segrave*, can best describe what then happened.

'There came a slight thud, and I looked up at Sir Henry, who

## 'Miss England II'

was sitting normally with both hands on the wheel. Yet both engines were switched off, spinning round losing momentum, and both clutches were out; we were coasting along to a standstill.

'Sir Henry said, "It's alright, I think we've broken something down aft. Prop shaft or something."

'Vic Halliwell said, "But you've got the clutches out!" and he and I just sat and goggled at each other in amazement; we were travelling at 107 m.p.h. at the time of the breakage. The clutches, one for each engine, were operated by two levers, one on either side of Sir Henry's seat. He had to let go the wheel, holding it between his knees, operate two switches, lean forward, grasp the levers, depress two knobs on the top, pull them towards him past the hips and some inches behind him, release the knobs and put his two hands on the wheel again – all in the fraction of time it takes a normal person to lift his head!

'I looked at the wake trailing away behind us; it was as straight as a die. I have sat in the seat of Miss England II many times since those days and marvelled. You see, it was not merely physical action in that fraction of a second – the senses had to realize that something was wrong, where it was, and the correct thing to do to prevent further damage, in a brand-new boat the second time out. It was hardly credible. One of the blades had broken off the two-bladed propeller while revolving at 12,000 r.p.m. – 200 revs per second – but think of the speed of those messages to the brain and limb!'

This graphic description is sufficient in itself to explain the man Segrave and his split-second reactions.

Propellers seemed to become, for some time, the *bête noir* of the new boat, and there ensued much experimenting with pitches and diameters. And the machining of these experimental screws proved to be costly in time, money and life. For one Saunders-Roe engineer was killed when a grinding wheel shattered in his face during a finishing grinding operation on one of the propellers.

Becoming impatient, and conscious that he was also keeping a lot of interested people waiting, Segrave on June 12th announced

## 'Auto'-Biography

that on the morrow he would either 'break the record or the propeller', and the following morning, Friday the 13th, I was down on the jetties very early, watching with some envy as launches and cruisers left the bay carrying pressmen and photographers to take up station along the measured mile. For, though Bertie Borwick had, as usual, put an old battered dinghy at my disposal, the strapping around my damaged rib prevented any serious rowing, and it seemed that I had no hope of watching the attempt at close quarters.

As I watched Miss England being eased down the slip, a voice called 'Hoi – young feller? You've grown a bit, haven't you?' and turning, I looked down into one of the launches which was about to leave the jetty on which I stood. Sitting grinning in the stern was my friend of the Irish Sea crossing some three years earlier. The same wispy moustache, the same horn-rimmed spectacles and certainly his rig of tweed cap and plus-fours looked the same. I returned his grin with delight as he indicated an empty seat and gestured to me to jump aboard. We shook hands and we chatted animatedly as the launch took us towards the measured mile. But even on this second meeting, we never exchanged names for some reason, and I repeat my earlier plea that, should he read this, he writes, 'phones or hollers to identify himself.

The skipper of our craft positioned it close to the west bank of the lake, almost at the centre of the mile and when, around 1 p.m., we heard Miss England's engines start up back in Bowness Bay, there was a scramble of passengers to the side of the launch nearest the course, causing us to list at an alarming angle. However, all was well – these sturdy, beamy Windermere-built boats can take a lot of roll.

Miss England came streaking up to the start of the mile, her wake fanning out in a sharply defined segment, and, as she passed our viewpoint, heading north, a secondary, lower wake was visible, caused, said my knowledgeable friend, by the exposed tips of the two propeller blades as they thrashed the water. We watched as the boat passed the end of the mile, and as she slowed her wake

*'Miss England II'*

became a cloud as she came off her planing wedge and settled on her hull bottom, the greater displacement disturbing the water.

That had certainly been a fast run, and we watched keenly as Segrave turned his craft and headed back for his return. For, as with the land speed record, two runs had to be effected in a record attempt, the average of the two being the speed recognized. And this time, as she creamed along the surface her speed seemed even faster and her wake more pronounced. Amateur timekeepers on our boat were sure that the record was in the bag, and that we could now head back to the boathouses to join in the celebrations. However, within seconds of Miss England passing the end of the mile there were shouts of 'She's coming back!' and once again we crowded the gunwale to watch her pass for the third time. Obviously Segrave felt that his boat had still more to offer in the way of speed, and was determined to clinch his record by a handsome margin.

Just as she passed us we heard a muffled thud and saw her bows start to snake rapidly from port to starboard, and her wake break up into an uneven pattern. Segrave, clearly visible to us, was wrestling with the wheel, still, apparently, with his throttles wide open. Briefly, the huge white craft straightened up, but then, in a fraction of a second, her bows rose high from the water and she flipped, with a strange corkscrew movement, on to her back.

Our boatman rushed to start our engine, but we were by no means first on the scene. By the time we reached the upturned and partially submerged craft, two of the team, Sir Henry and Wilcocks, had been snatched from the water, after one spectator had dived fully clothed to the rescue. Sir Henry was rushed to a house on the west bank, Belle Grange, where, with Lady Segrave sitting at his bedside, he died some two and a half hours later, after anxiously inquiring about his colleagues and about his record.

We later learned that the injuries from which he succumbed included two broken arms, two broken ribs, a crushed thigh and a perforated lung. Vic Halliwell, dead, was later recovered from the water, and Wilcocks suffered a badly torn leg.

## 'Auto'-Biography

We also learned more of the greatness of this modest, kindly man later, when other information came to hand. He had ordered three armoured life-jackets for use on the record attempt, but, because only one had arrived at Windermere, he declined it rather than take an unfair advantage over his team-mates. And, had he jumped from his cockpit when Miss England started to gyrate, he may well have saved his own life. But, deliberately, he stayed at the wheel, keeping the power on in order to give himself some degree of control and his two engineers a chance of survival.

Sir Henry and Miss England II secured their record, their average speed being 98·76 m.p.h.

As I type these words, I sit at my study window, from which I can look out over the lake to the very spot where it all happened, and I recall how we all marvelled at the sheer speed of the boat. Thirty-nine years ago it seemed phenomenal, but I was to see history repeat itself when far greater speeds were involved. But of that – later.

By the time the inquest was held, I was home again, but I studied the findings carefully. The coroner suggested that Miss England had probably struck an object floating in her path, and a three-foot length of waterlogged tree branch was shown in the court. It bore fresh scars and had been found in the vicinity of the crash. The hull had been ruptured, the planing step had partially left its mountings and the resultant drag had caused the boat to overturn. The verdict was 'accidental death'.

But the talk around the boatyards was not about a partially submerged tree branch; it was about the mounting of the planing step to the hull; the manner by which – in order to be adjustable – it was secured to the boat. Was the method adequate to cope with the immense stresses imposed? Had it been sufficiently well tested at progressively higher speeds? Whatever the answers, the subject is one which still causes heated discussion in certain circles within two miles of my home. So fresh is the subject in the minds of certain people, that the accident could have happened but yesterday.

CHAPTER SIX

# *In which father changes course*

Some weeks after my return from the Lake District father finally severed all links with the firm to which he had been so devoted, and which had employed him for so many years. The severance hurt him badly and he seemed to retire into a shell of despondency, speaking only in monosyllables and with the habitual smile absent from his face. Even the fact that another cricket season was with us failed to arouse any spark of enthusiasm. He refused very tempting offers of jobs with the erstwhile rivals, Leyland's; offers which, had he accepted would have put him on a very sound footing financially. Many of his colleagues had joined Leyland, and brother Tommy had gone into their publicity office, but despite their joint efforts to persuade him to join them, father resisted. He intended, he said, to go it alone, and, as though this decision had suddenly sparked off a new lease of life he came out of his blues and became, to some extent, his own cheerful self once more.

Perhaps with an eye to my future he decided to look for a suitable garage business in the vicinity of Southport and to this end was offered the backing of a wealthy friend, whose profits from a chain of drapery shops throughout Lancashire permitted him to indulge in a stable of personal cars. And, as though his offer of financial backing were not enough, he capped this by lending father one of his cars to aid his search of the district, an offer gratefully accepted as the 'Leaf' had gone with the Vulcan job.

I have no doubt that when the generous-hearted 'Teddy' told father to select a car from the stable of four which consisted of a 1924 Austin Seven tourer, a 1927 Austin Seven graced by a 'Bill' Lyons Swallow body created in the neighbouring town of Blackpool, a Bentley of unknown age and a car bearing a name as

## 'Auto'-Biography

delightful as the machine itself – 'Alfa Romeo', he fully expected him to choose one of the Austins. And it must indeed have been a severe test of friendship when father unhesitatingly opted for the Italian beauty. Teddy must have been a very worried man that day as he watched us drive away from his home, for this particular model had only been catalogued during the previous year and had only been in Teddy's possession for two months.

The Alfa opened my eyes to the existence of the exotics in the world of motoring, and gave me a close up of a marque which previously had been a feature of the racing scene to be viewed from a distance only. The model was the Gran Sport 1750 c.c. two-seater, with six-cylinder, twin overhead camshaft, Roots 'blown' engine. And what a gem of a car it was. Long, lean and completely uncluttered by any unnecessary embellishment, with sweeping, flared front wings and high running boards, and with classic radiator sloping gently backwards. Wire wheels, knock-off hub caps, massive brake drums; the whole emitting an aura of sheer power.

My motoring reading habits ensured that I knew my Alfa 'gen'. I knew that the initials ALFA stood for Amonima Lombardo Fabrica Automobili, and that the suffix Romeo was the surname of an engineer who had taken over the firm after the First World War. I knew that drivers with such names as Ascari, Campari and Brilli-Peri had wrought stirring deeds with Alfas and that the marque had won numerous Grands Prix and had taken the 1925 World Championship. But this was Alfa lore in general. What I did not know about this particular car was why Teddy had bought it. It was an out and out sports car with racing potential, yet the only car he drove personally from his stable was the old Austin Seven; his chauffeur drove the others. Perhaps it was sheer joy of possession or a spot of one-upmanship.

Whatever his reason, here it was, and here I was, sitting in the very confined quarters of the narrow cockpit as father quietly drove it home, he familiarizing himself with the feel of the car, and I basking in reflected glory as we passed some school pals and I saw

## In which father changes course

undiluted envy written on their faces. If ever there was a time for the regal wave, this was it.

I recall to mind little of the search for a garage business which ensued over the next ten days, but I certainly remember the Alfa in which the search was conducted. I accompanied father each day on his trips throughout a thirty-mile radius of the town, and looked forward each morning to tickling the Memini carburettor before climbing into my seat and awaiting the pressing of the starter button. This small movement would spark off, for me, a sound of music, for the six-cylinder engine had a sound unlike any other I had heard, the burble from the exhaust, increasing to a rasp as more throttle was applied, being pure joy to the ear. Father also enjoyed the car, although I remember he did not like the steering characteristics. In deference to Teddy, and because we did not have then the fine multi-laned highways leading to and from the town, he never drove the Alfa above sixty miles per hour but even at that speed he had to learn to give the steering its head to the extent of permitting the wheel to slip through his fingers as the front wheels encountered pot-holes. For he had quickly realized that, should he grip the wheel too tightly, the car would slide without warning, even on a dry surface.

As for me, my job was to watch the instruments on the facia which lurked beneath a cowling; tucked away in such a strange manner that the driver had to duck his head to read them with the consequent risk of striking his chin on the steering wheel boss.

Only one business was for sale in the town at that time, and unfortunately the asking price was well outside the limit imposed by father's backer. I say unfortunately because this same business is the nucleus from which has grown a large Lancashire group, which thrives, holds important franchises and enjoys a reputation for quality and fair dealing. So the search went out into the country roads in the district, father looking at garages whose owners promptly raised their price when they saw the Alfa. One such garage, near the village of Rufford on what was the then main Southport to Preston road, father liked, and after much haggling a price was agreed with the vendor. However, on the very day when father was due at his solicitor's office to sign the contract of purchase, some instinct sent him to the offices of the Lancashire County Council at Preston. There he learned that a new highway was to be constructed to link Southport with Preston and the north, and, after studying the plans with a helpful official, he realized that the road would completely by-pass the garage and that insufficient traffic would then be passing to provide it with an income.

No doubt the owner knew all about the road, and no doubt this was his reason for selling. But he 'forgot' to mention it and father, the soul of integrity himself, and completely naïve in his inability to spot a lack of this virtue in others, was disgusted at what he called 'damned sharp practice'. And from this point he began to cool off. After 'tearing a considerable strip' from the would-be vendor his interest in the garage, or any other, waned. The Alfa, to my sorrow, was restored to its owner – no doubt much to his relief – and for the first time in my young life, we were a family without a car.

Perhaps now, we thought, father would join the Henry Spurrier team at Leyland, having got the wish to be self-employed out of his system. But how wrong we were, for some weeks after the garage incident, he succumbed to what we and his many friends could only suppose was a rush of blood to the head.

During a two mile walk to church one Sunday morning, a fellow choir member who joined us, casually informed father that a shop we were passing was for sale. Father stopped in his tracks, stared at the corner shop which was graced by a Victorian glass veranda, and then marched up to its windows, into which he gazed for several seconds. He looked at mother, who wore a puzzled expression, and then he continued at a brisk walk to church, some few hundred yards away. Mother stared at Tommy, then at me, and simultaneously we all said 'Oh no!'

During the ensuing few weeks, events tumbled over each other. Father, in the face of heated protest from the family, and against the advice of his friends, bought the business and leased the house

## In which father changes course

which went with it. Whenever he had pulled off crazy stunts in the past, he had always had the complete support of mother, Tommy and me, for they always stemmed from his keen sense of fun and usually resulted in something hilarious. But this time we were all convinced that his senses had left him entirely. For a man whose working life had been spent amongst machinery, and for so many years had been devoted to transport; a man who was recognized unstintingly throughout his own sphere as a brilliant engineer, to suddenly make a complete break from a job he loved to become a small shopkeeper, seemed to us to be utterly mad, and our loyalty to the 'old man' was placed under severe strain. Loyalty however won the day for father. Our old home was sold and we moved into the house attached to the shop.

The shop's stock, taken over at valuation, seemed to consist of everything under the sun, from drawing-pins to bacon, from postage-stamps to keg-butter. There were glass-fronted display cabinets in abundance, all crammed with goods, edible and inedible. There was a long row of glass-lidded biscuit tins wherein lurked the products of Mr McVitie and Mr Crawford. And one object particularly intrigued me; a bacon-slicing machine with a huge, lethal-looking, razor-sharp cutting disc. Perhaps, I thought, this was going to be fun after all, especially as my favourite scent – that of freshly ground coffee beans – pervaded the whole of the shop.

When father held a 'committee meeting' with us all one evening and told us his plans, we all began to feel that perhaps he was not so daft after all. And when he explained that his plans included the purchase of another car, I at least was finally won over.

If all those plans had reached fruition, father may well have become another Sainsbury, with a chain of super-markets. However, like so many other ideas which sound good in theory, they were destined to come unstuck in practice. He felt that all his many friends, his numerous relatives and the congregation of the church would all rally round him and willingly change their regular source of supply for the pleasure of buying from him; that the shop should

## '*Auto*'-*Biography*

not be so dependent on its local customers and that he could make regular deliveries throughout the town and even to the more distant towns where friends and relations abounded.

I could fill the pages of another book with descriptions of how these grandiose plans went awry; how father failed to cost his telephone calls and motoring expenses against the abysmal profits he made; how the weekly visits to the shop of chauffeured Rolls-Royce and Humber limousines looked very impressive but only succeeded in the end in driving away the local custom, on which, despite father's theory, the shop really depended for survival. The primary object of this particular book, however, is to describe the cars which have passed through my life, and certainly during the few years when we were shopkeepers, there was a great variety of these, each of them having a character, good or positively evil, of its very own.

The first, and the one which coincided with the red-letter day when I acquired my first driving licence, was a Standard Twelve, some seven or eight years old when father bought it for the princely sum of £35. Its awful colour, immediately obvious, and its vicious temper, which I discovered in due course, were jointly responsible for the name by which we came to know it – 'The Yellow Peril'. I lost count of the number of times I trapped my fingers in the Heath Robinson type framework of the canvas hood when raising or lowering it. And this was a frequent operation which depended entirely on the vagaries of the weather. In rain, that hood would be as taut as a drum-skin, but when dry it sagged to such an extent that it touched the heads of the driver and passengers. I am sure that car took an instant dislike to me from the moment we first met. In addition to the finger trapping it would, no matter how carefully I adjusted the ignition or held the starting handle, kick me like a fractious colt, especially early in the morning when I was in no mood for that kind of thing. The engine would die on me at the most awkward moments, and although it was furnished with a self-starter, it never did, if you know what I mean. This unit would choose the moment of my embarrassment to mal-

*In which father changes course*

function also, which meant that I had to get out and swing the damned thing, to the intense amusement of any friend who happened to pass. Of punctures there were plenty, although in fairness I did not hold these against the old car. I was well versed in punctures and they were a common enough hazard to the motoring of those days.

To be scrupulously fair about the old Yellow Peril, it never did let me down to any major extent on its longer week-end runs. We would set off on a Saturday morning, loaded to the gunwales with cardboard boxes of groceries, after the customary argument with the starting handle, and after a careful study of the heavens for a clue as to whether it was to be an 'up' day or a 'down' day for the hood, and set our sights on Bolton and the homes of our many relatives. We had a choice of two routes for the thirty odd mile journey; the flat route via Chorley and the hilly one via Parbold. The decision as to which we took depended entirely on the early morning mood of the engine. If the big and little end noises were synchronizing well with the tappets, we chose Parbold, confident that we should safely reach the summit. If however there was discord in the percussion section, with numbers one and four big ends trying to drown out numbers two and three little ends, then we would opt for the Chorley route. Being more popularly used it possessed more wayside garages than the other in case trouble developed. But there was seldom any real trouble, and once hot the Standard engine would slog along all day.

In spite of any redeeming features it may have had, I never grew fond of the beast, and the only claim it could possibly have on my affections was the fact that, because of it, I met the girl who five years later became my wife. Rollo and I had been to a variety show at a local theatre one evening, to listen to George Formby's crude ditties, and after the show we came out to find a snowstorm raging. We made a dash for the Yellow Peril parked nearby, and of course this proved to be one more occasion when the self-starter failed to function. As I struggled with the crank, snow beating down my neck, Rollo decided to perform one of his Sir

79

## *'Auto'-Biography*

Galahad acts. Two attractive girls, whom he had spotted staring with dismay at the snow from the theatre doorway, were invited to 'Hop in and we'll run you home!' The blighter certainly took a risk that night – those girls may well have lived in Wagga Wagga. All was well, however, they were Southport girls and, after looking doubtfully at the car and at the odd sight of me, perspiring heavily in a snowstorm, they decided to risk accepting the lift. Thus I met Bunny, of whom more anon.

The shop's trading results in the first few months encouraged father. Certainly his friends and relatives supported him, until the novelty wore off and they returned to their previous suppliers. Such was his early enthusiasm that to persuade him to exchange the Standard for something better proved easy, and I was instructed to look around to see what was on the market. Some of his initial keenness for the shop rubbed off on to me, and I began to think that perhaps there was a future in it. I was coming to the end of my schooldays, with any thought of further education having been squashed by the demise of the Vulcan and father's reduced income. The shop seemed to offer some sort of promise, and, putting aside any thoughts I had been cherishing of becoming an engineer, and having been granted a comparatively free hand, I decided that the shop should acquire a status symbol to advertise its success and prosperity, in the shape of a car of some distinction. I began to 'shop around' the motor trade, and I knew just what I was looking for.

Of all the cars which had passed through father's hands, the one that had impressed me the most – with the exception of Teddy's Alfa – was the little Riley Monaco, which had remained in his keeping for such a short time; certainly too short a time for me to really drive it on the roads. True, I had enjoyed one or two illicit spins without the legal blessing of a driver's licence, and I had certainly derived much pleasure from the beach driving. But this was not the same as being able to drive with a clear conscience, wherever and whenever I wanted. This model was now four years old and second-hand examples were beginning to

13. Dignity and impudence, Austin Seven chases Lagonda at Southport in the thirties

14. T. L. Moss in the M.G. Magna gets the flag as the winner of the fifteen-mile race at Southport, 1933

*In which father changes course*

appear in the advertisements and the showrooms. I determined to find one, and succeeded.

Prices of second-hand cars, even in the Southport of those days, were considerably higher than in nearby Liverpool, and knowing this, I took the Standard to the city one evening and did a comprehensive tour of all the showrooms and trading yards. I found three Riley Monacos, two of which were showing very high mileages on their 'clocks' and looking very tatty and uncared for. In the third, which was tucked away behind some much more impressive machinery, I found exactly what I wanted. The car had obviously been recently repainted in a green which I supposed was British Racing; the interior was unblemished and the seating uncreased. It was first registered in 1927 and, if I could believe the mileage registered, it seemed to represent an average of 5,000 per year since new. Without even starting the engine I asked the salesman the price. He was busy picking his teeth in a bored sort of way, and only paused to murmur 'A hunnerd an' fifty. Bin a doctor's bus an' it's a good 'un' before resuming his self scavenging operation.

'What will you give me for the Standard?'

'What Standard?'

'The one outside.'

He walked to the showroom window outside which I had parked the Yellow Peril; he stared through the glass at the car; he bent down and peered more closely, and, without going outside to look at the car, turned to me and muttered 'Fifty quid.'

Fifty quid! And father had paid thirty-five some three or four thousand miles earlier. Either father had got a bargain or this fellow was off his rocker. I made a hasty decision and asked if I could use his telephone. Permission granted I put through a call to home and put father fully in the picture.

'What's the Riley like?' he asked.

'Perfect – it's a pippin.'

'Engine?'

'Er – I haven't tried it.'

## 'Auto'-Biography

'Well, try it, you chump, and 'phone me back.'

The engine, on choke, started immediately and I let it warm up until, choke pushed in, it ticked over like a clock. Oil pressure good and battery charging. Lights all working, screenwiper scraping noisily over the dry glass. Two minutes tick over and then I stabbed the accelerator, looking to the rear of the car. No blue smoke. No smoke at all. Must be good.

And so it proved. The following afternoon father accompanied me back to Liverpool and the deal was effected.

I have gone to some length in describing this, my first experience with the gentlemen of the motor trade. For the particular example with whom I dealt with is now a director of the large firm which grew up from the small one in which we met. His suitings are now as immaculate as the wares he sells, and, as our paths cross from time to time, I often wonder if he too looks back at those days, and wonders how he got where he is.

As I type these pages I learn from a press release that British Leyland are to phase out the Riley name; that production is to cease. The reason given is that Rileys account for less than one per cent of the country's registrations, and they state that the decision has been reached 'only after very careful consideration'. I would argue with them that the consideration should have been given to the Riley many years before; that the blame for having to phase out such a famous marque must rest firmly on the shoulders of executives past and present. And their treatment of the Riley Nine is one example of where they came adrift in their thinking. For as the Nine which commenced with the Monaco became, over the years, progressively more handsome, and with its added embellishments, very much heavier, its engine power failed to keep up with it. Ronald Barker, writing about Rileys in the *Autocar* of August 1967 put the matter far more succinctly than this when he wrote: 'The design advanced on the flanks, so to speak, but not in the middle, and ultimately it was overtaken by previously humble rivals.'

Having jumped well ahead in time to ventilate my protest, I

*In which father changes course*

must now return to the days when Rileys were very much a part of the contemporary motoring scene. But I shall take up my cudgels again, for I feel very strongly that to add this famous name to the long list of motoring's lost causes is nothing less than a crime against those of us who still retain a spot of romance in our make-up. Think again, Lord Stokes; let not the needs of your export drive exclude we who, however indirectly, helped you to build your empire.

The first thing I did with the Riley was to personalize it by having a thin gold line painted along the waistline. This at once broke up the somewhat slab-sided look of the car. (Thirty-seven years later I note that owners are giving the same treatment to their Austin and Morris 1100/1300 cars.) The next move was to 'scrub out' thoroughly the engine compartment, and to polish everything which would polish. After painting, in aluminium enamel, the five brass nuts securing each wheel to its hub, I felt I then had my 'car of distinction'. The side lights, surmounting the flared front wings, and the headlights, located on the wing valances, were unfortunately stove enamelled in black, and I could do nothing about that. In those days, plating was an expensive and tricky business, and I no longer had the facilities of the Vulcan workshops at my disposal. However, I was well satisfied with my Monaco, and ready to do some serious motoring.

CHAPTER SEVEN

# *Roman orgy*

For a while it seemed that my theory of looking successful in order to ensure success, was paying off; that the sight of the smart little Riley buzzing around the town, either making deliveries or collecting fresh stocks from the wholesalers, attracted more and more custom to the shop. And certainly the fact that some of the 'leading ladies' from the top social class patronized Ernie Knowles's shop was sufficient in itself to attract many lesser lights, who came in the belief that such patronage was obviously the currently done thing.

For the Southport of those days was just as conscious of, and anxious to be seen doing the done thing, as the Southport of today. I feel sure that Miss Mitford, when researching for her treatise on matters 'U' and 'non-U' must have used Southport as her base, and I am quite sure that her published work found many subscribers in the town. (My wife and I chortled recently when, reading through a copy of the town's local paper, we saw that one of the socialites was quoted as saying to an interviewer that 'Of course I never serve chicken to my dinner guests – it is simply not done', and, having chortled, we promptly went out to buy a chicken.)

In due course we were to learn that the initial success of the business was but a passing phase, promoted primarily by the loyalty and sympathy of friends and relations, and further boosted by the curiosity of the upper crust. Neither father nor I were ever cut out to be tycoons; we lacked the ability to 'see around the corner'. However, in the belief that we had a winner on our hands, it was agreed that my working week should be so arranged that my weekends would be free, and that I could thus pursue my favourite subject, motor sport. My 'country' and long-distance deliveries were now effected in the evenings, leaving Saturday and Sunday for the watching of, and participation in racing, rallying and hill-climbing.

I watched such drivers as Campbell, Birkin and Kaye Don driving Bentleys, Delages, Alfas and Bugattis, at such venues as Phoenix Park, the Isle of Man and Brooklands, and I never missed a race meeting on our own beach, where, from drivers whom I came to know well, I scrounged as many rides as I possibly could.

Having joined a newly formed west Lancashire club, I helped in organizing, and participating in, rallies and hill-climbs. All on an amateur footing, of course, but good fun nonetheless. In their planning our rallies were somewhat scrappy, and would most certainly have been frowned on by the august RAC. We had few checkpoints on our chosen routes, as most of our members preferred to drive or navigate rather than stand around in draughty, outlandish spots holding charts and stop-watches. And our handicapping system was somewhat rough and ready, based as it was on the horse-power of the competing cars, whereby cars such as my Riley would start off early in the list, preceded only by such cars as Austin Sevens and the little beauty which belonged to a particular pal of mine, 'Bill' Stewart. This was an 847 c.c. M-type MG Midget, a car I coveted greatly.

Last to start in our rallies would be nothing less than a 1927 $4\frac{1}{2}$-litre Bentley tourer which was driven by the son of a wealthy Liverpool tea merchant, and, for the benefit of those whose eyes lit up at the mention of the word, this Bentley was the machine with the four-cylinder engine which developed something around 110 b.h.p. and had a top speed of some 92 m.p.h. This was the 'unblown' version, but I believe I am correct in saying that forty or fifty of them were supercharged with a Roots blower, and thus developed 182 b.h.p. to give a top speed of 105 m.p.h. I certainly know that this model is much revered and sought after by Bentley connoisseurs.

The Bentley gave lustre to our humble club, but I am afraid

## 'Auto'-Biography

that the driver was only tolerated because of his car. He had a depressing habit of talking about his cottage at Trearddur Bay, on Anglesey; about his two sailing dinghies, his father's 'other cars' and about his apparently superabundant girl friends. Depressing because most of us seemed to run our cars on shoestrings and could boast of only one girl friend. As I knew the chap as a result of his frequent visits to the shop, selling his father's 'special blended', and had introduced him to the club, I was the one at the receiving end of the sour looks whenever he started sounding off. He was my protegé – could I not shut him up? I could not, and it was to take one of our rallies to quieten him down, with the result that he became quite a decent fellow.

We had planned quite an ambitious November rally which our type-written newsletter described as 'The Bonfire Night Rally'. Our route would take us through the night to Preston, the wild moorland of the Trough of Bowland and from thence to the Lake District, where, after a sortie over the Wrynose and Hardknott Passes, we planned to gather for a pre-dawn picnic at the Roman fort on Hardknott. There we would set off fireworks, before setting off again for Keswick and a fast, main road run home. We did not have a single check point, and we took each other entirely on trust, taking only one precaution against any driver who may feel tempted to 'skip' the Trough route and to press on to Hardknott via the main road north. Bill Stewart and I had realized just how easy it would be for any scoundrel to do just this, and thus gain a better placing in the final results. We therefore telephoned 'Tom', mine host of the club's favourite pub in the Trough, and extracted a promise from him that he would keep his outside light on all night. In return, we promised, the club would pay him a visit in the near future and keep his beer pumps busy. We felt that at least we should have a rough check on the competitors at the end of the rally by being able to ask them 'was Tom's light on or off?' And our ploy seemed to work well enough for, when we did eventually perform our inquisition, one wretch was caught out and had to admit he had missed out the Trough section, and had pressed

## Roman orgy

on through Lancaster. Not, he assured us, in order to gain a better placing, but because his gearbox had become noisy. We gave him the benefit of the doubt, and promptly disqualified him.

That was a splendid and memorable rally. To even up the numbers 'sex-wise' each driver was asked to take his girl friend along as navigator, or, should he not have a girl, then to find one and bring her along. This resulted in most of the four-seater cars having a complement of at least four people, the prospect of a Roman orgy on the summit of Hardknott attracting passengers who were not club members, but who, enthusiasts after the event, were certainly to join us.

Seventeen cars of all shapes and sizes, and in various states of roadworthiness, started off that night, all loaded with spare petrol, sandwiches, vacuum flasks of coffee, bottled beer and a contribution to the promised firework display. In each front seat sat a blonde or brunette. The whole effect, I thought as I walked the line before the start, checking all the entrants, looked very cosy. The tail-ender, our friend whom I shall call 'Special Blend'; our friend of the Bentley, had obviously been greedy. He had brought two girls along. Typical, I thought. I had plucked up enough courage to ask Bunny, the girl whom I had met on the night of the snowstorm, to join me as my navigator, and she, exhibiting even greater courage, accepted.

Starting off in fifth position on my handicap, I gradually worked my way past three assorted 'sevens' until I had the tail-lights of Bill's MG in view. This stationing was always pre-arranged between us, and we would maintain it throughout a rally, only 'dicing' at the closing stages if we had a chance of winning. In effect we acted as support cars, one to the other, in case of trouble.

Preston was negotiated, its citizens on their way to bed, and we set our sights on the Trough. Through the Ribble valley, through Whalley and into the bleak, winding and undulating roads which traverse the foothills of the western Pennines. My driving mirror told me that the pack was in full cry behind me. We had no quartziodine lamps with which to supplement our somewhat inadequate lighting in those days, but the beams from the following headlights were impressive enough as they stabbed the night sky, rising and falling like wartime searchlights. This was good, this was rallying.

Passing Tom's pub, we acknowledged his illuminated inn-sign with a gentle bleep from our horns, and reached a point roughly half way through the Trough. Here I began to feel a bit anxious, for I knew that Bill would shortly pull into the side of the road and stop, and that he would expect me to fall in behind. And I knew his purpose, for this too was regular practice. He and I had solved the rally driver's problem of disposing of surplus fluid, by using a given spot on a given route, and on this route that spot happened to be a certain tree. My anxiety stemmed from the fact that tonight I had a new navigator, unaccustomed to crude rallying types, and, when Bill did stop and I stopped behind him, I sat for a few seconds puzzling how best to explain to Bunny the reason for the night-halt.

'Trouble?' she asked.

'Er – no. This is our tree.'

'Ah – your tree,' she replied, as though realization had dawned, or the penny dropped. But it hadn't, for she still gave me a quizzical look. At that point in my dilemma, Bill's constant girl friend and regular navigator, Jean, came up to us, grinned at Bunny and beckoned with her finger. The two girls vanished into the undergrowth on one side of the road, and Bill and I paid our compliments to the tree on the other. I have passed that spot many times in later years, marvelled at the lushness of that spinney, and like to think that Bill and I made our contributions to that lushness.

As we performed our ritual, the fact that other cars passed us never caused us concern. Although their drivers would usually shout raucous comments, we knew that, unless they had inbuilt toilet facilities in their own cars, they too would have to stop somewhere, and we should gradually resume our respective positions. And anyway, it wasn't a race. It was just damned good fun.

So the Trough section was completed, and we started on the main road sprint to Milnthorpe, where, half way up the steep and

## Roman orgy

grinding hill which leads out of the town, we found ourselves baulked by a ship's propeller of all things. Of tremendous height and diameter, this phosphor-bronze monster positively leered at us as the driver of its transporter struggled to find a still lower gear. These propellers were always a hazard to be expected on this stretch of road during darkness. Wisely, they were transported from their factory of origin in the midlands to the shipyards of the Clyde, at night, in order to minimize inconvenience to other road users. Unfortunately the same wisdom is not always applied today when 'abnormal' loads are moved. Usually we would encounter such a load at a spot where passing was possible, but this time, having met up with it here, we knew we were in for a long, long crawl before the road would widen sufficiently to permit us to go ahead.

It mattered little; it was part of the fun of the game. But due to the delay, it meant that as we eventually passed through the hamlet of Little Langdale and commenced the traverse of the Wrynose Pass, the first tentative shafts of dawn were lighting the fells to the east, and I had doubts as to the effectiveness of our proposed firework display if daylight caught us up too soon.

Wrynose today is not an ideal touring road. Passing places are few and the surface indifferent, varying as it does between tarmac and concrete. In the thirties it was even worse, and I was always a little anxious about some of our newer members whose driving ability and nerve were still unknown quantities. All was well on this occasion, however, and as we passed the Three Shire Stone (where Lancashire, Westmorland and Cumberland meet), just below the summit Bunny turned in her seat and assured me that she could count twelve sets of headlights probing the road behind us. As I was in fifth position I knew our original number was still intact.

At Cockley Beck, where Wrynose continues through the Duddon valley to the left, and the ascent of Hardknott, which leads to Eskdale, commences on the right, there was a compulsory stop. Here, we always briefed newcomers to Hardknott on the problem confronting them, and insisted that any who doubted his car's

## 'Auto'-Biography

ability or his own should take the Duddon road, and to regard his part of the rally ended. There were seldom any takers of this latter suggestion, and certainly there were none on this occasion.

Hardknott is a fascinating driving experience. Even the Maakinens, the Moss-Carlssons and the Hopkirks of today's RAC Rallies will admit to this. The sheer steepness of the pass – one in three in places – and its multi-hairpins are a challenge even to today's skilful drivers. In the thirties this challenge was even greater, especially to a motley collection of mostly ageing cars, such as those owned by our members. These were the 'blue smoke' days when piston rings seemed to avoid their proper function and permitted oil to reach the 'top of the pots'; days when gear ratios, power to weight ratios and crown wheels and pinions were liable to be found wanting at the most inconvenient moments. Days when clutch plates juddered, transmission shafts whipped and fabric 'universals' tended to come unstuck. So our Hardknott climbs were always interesting; always good for a laugh and occasionally dramatic.

This was one of our luckier nights. The cars commenced the climb at intervals, and the sombre fells were lit by the flicker of the headlights. The Riley was in top form and I listened with an aesthetic pleasure to the sporty sound of its exhaust as we bottom geared through the first three hairpins, keeping well to the wrong side of the road to avoid any possibility of side slipping into the awesome gorges to our left. As I approached the fourth hairpin, climbing hard, I was suddenly confronted with a stalled car, and had to stand on my brake pedal, rasp up the handbrake lever and stop dead in my tracks. Switching off and leaving the car in bottom gear, I told Bunny to warn the following drivers with her torch, and walked up to Ken Walton's Austin Seven tourer. I found Ken and his girl friend sitting, arms folded, singing away at the tops of their voices.

'S'matter Ken?'

'Did you pass an engine on your way up, old boy? I think mine's dropped out. Either that, or I've lost my touch.'

Ken's girl assured me that he had not lost his touch, though I doubt if she spoke in the same context.

There was usually an answer to the problem of running out of steam in bottom gear, for there was still one more gear to go. With the help of another team from a following car we lifted the Austin bodily, turned it round in the opposite direction, and gave Ken his instructions.

'Now – into reverse – and up you go!'

And so he did, he and his passenger laughing their heads off as they drove backwards up Hardknott. That he left his confounded headlights on and blinded me as I followed, was apparently of little consequence.

So we surmounted the summit, and began the descent through the hairpins on the Eskdale side until we reached the comparatively level turf in the vicinity of the Roman Camp which is now called Hardknott Castle, and, in the far off days of its building, MEDIOBOGDVM. Here, with room on one side of the road or the other, for us all to park, we counted heads. Seventeen had started out and seventeen had reached the fort. Not bad for an amateur club with no supporting facilities.

At the tumbled stones of the ancient fort – not then as carefully restored as they are today – we first allocated two walls to the two sexes as 'necessaria', and then began to unpack our gear. One member had brought along a portable gramophone, and there, where Agricola's soldiery had slept, eaten, drilled and watched over the marches from the sea, we of another era danced to 'Mood Indigo', drank our coffee and our beer. And the huge masses of Hardknott Fell and Raven Crag still resisted the light of a new day, and set a wonderful back-cloth to our firework display.

What the Friends of the Lake District, the National Trust and the Ministry of Works would have said about our goings-on in the early hours of that November morning, I shudder to think. I now have many friends amongst the members of those august bodies, and, should they read this, I am sure they will let me know.

## 'Auto'-Biography

We had some splendid fun and left behind us not a scrap of litter. I like to think that the ghosts of Agricola's legions which may still people that remote old fortress looked benignly upon our orgy that morning. After all, they knew all about these things, didn't they?

I have dwelt lengthily on a description of our Bonfire Night Rally with one purpose in mind; to explain how, thanks to a pyrotechnical misadventure, the bore who was Special Blend and was only tolerated because of his Bentley, became a decent chap and a popular member. And I must press on with my explanation.

After a splendid show of fireworks, during which Roman candles predominated, of course, and which must have caused the slumbering cottagers far below in Eskdale to awaken, and to suppose that the soldiery had returned, we placed a large rocket in an empty beer bottle, intending it to soar high above the fort as a signing-off gesture. A match was struck and applied; the touch paper sizzled and spluttered and we all stood well back to enjoy the full effect. Just as the rocket started to exhaust and we waited for it to launch itself skyward, the bottle tilted and, on a flat trajectory, the rocket sped unerringly for the spot where Special Blend sat in the rear seat of the Bentley, drinking the last of his beer.

That rocket fell right into his lap, from whence it continued to blast out its contents viciously. Special Blend emitted a bansheelike wail, leapt from his car and, hands flailing at his trousers, jumped face downwards into a beck which tumbles down to its meeting place with the River Esk below.

The delirious howl which went up from all sides had to be heard to be believed. We 'rolled in the aisles' so to speak and, to add to the poor chap's discomfiture, his two girl friends disloyally added their laughter to ours.

The run back home that day, back through the Lake District and so on to the main road south, was something of an anticlimax. Special Blend, after his soaking in the beck, had been kitted out with an odd assortment of spare clothing provided by sundry

## Roman orgy

members, and, by mutual agreement, we let him win the rally by a series of hurriedly and secretly contrived ploys. After all if we intended our events to be fun, then we had certainly achieved our intention on this one.

Although the symbols of it were undoubtedly scorched and probably smoke blackened, Special Blend's manhood was, fortunately, unimpaired. The damage was shared between his trousers and his dignity. But the resultant change to his personality was astonishing. Never again did he bore with his boasting, or, if ever a hint of it did creep into a conversation, it was enough for someone to murmur 'light the blue touch paper and retire smartly', for him to pause, grin, and change the subject.

Before I leave the subject of our club and our doings, I must tell of one event which ended less happily, and from which we all returned home in deflated mood.

Although, in the privacy of our club meetings, we always referred to our more ambitious motoring programme as consisting of 'rallies' or 'hill-climbs', these were terms we never used when speaking to outsiders. We had, after all, such matters as insurance policies, parental watchfulness and the awe-inspiring authority of 'the lor' to consider. At the mere mention of the word rally, our policies seemed suddenly to become invalid, and the other two symbols of power tended to frown severely at anything resembling sport which took place on public roads. Certainly we had no affiliation to or sponsorship by the RAC, although we had ambitions to be recognized by that body in due course, and thus to be able to shelter beneath their umbrella. Our immediate answer however, was to call all our events – whether they entailed beating along main roads at high speed, or snarling our way up steep gradients – 'treasure hunts', a blanket term we felt was less likely to incur the wrath of the 'antis', and a term which did not seem to figure amongst the small print which listed banned usage on our insurance policies.

The Bonfire Night Rally, organized and planned by Bill Stewart and I, had been such a success, and had met with such unanimous

*'Auto'-Biography*

acclaim from our members, that, by mutual consent they appointed us planners of all future events, and we thoroughly enjoyed the 'recces' we undertook to find suitable venues, the two of us usually sharing either the Riley or the MG in order to save expense. During one such recce, again in the Lake District – an area which drew us like a magnet because of its utter dissimilarity to the flat plain on which we lived – we discovered the perfect spot for a hill-climb meeting. And the route we travelled in order to reach it, guaranteed, by the very sportiness of its terrain, the complete approval of all competitors.

This is not a guide book to the Lakes, but, as I still consider this motoring route to be the finest in the district; its panoramic and restrospective views surpassing, in my opinion, any other, for the benefit of both 'familiar' and newcomer, I will describe it briefly.

Leaving Ambleside by the aptly named 'Struggle', which winds steeply out of the town and emerges at the summit of Kirkstone – where stands 'the highest inn in England' – proceed down the Pass to Brotherswater, and then to Patterdale and Glenridding. Drive then the full length of the Ullswater western shoreline, stopping frequently – unless you are rallying – for backward glances at some of the most delightful mountain scenery in the country. Reaching Pooley Bridge at the northernmost end of the lake, take the road along its eastern shore until you reach the foot of a splendid, steep, many hairpinned climb which leads from Howtown, up through the vale of Martin Dale, with Hollin Fell on the right and Steel Knotts on the left.

This Shelsley in miniature, unnamed to my knowledge, was the venue for our hill-climb; now a popular summer picnicking area, but little known in our young day, and a road which offered a challenge to our skills and a test for our gearboxes. We planned our event for a Saturday in the early spring which followed our Roman Camp winter venture, and once again we timed our arrival at the site for the hours just before dawn. What we planned to do was, we knew, highly irregular but we felt reasonably safe from

## Roman orgy

opposition by holding our competition at first light, before the 'natives' were awake.

We had no electronic starting 'wedge' with which to time our climbs, and had only one stop-watch between us. The answer then was to turn the climb into a 'circuit', whereby the cars would storm the hill, press on down the other side, and, turning at the ancient church in Martindale, return by the same route to the starting point. By this means the one stop-watch could be employed, and the return of the car would automatically inform the next competitor that his road was clear. We stationed one of the girls in the party on the flanks of Hollin Fell, from where she had a view of the full circuit, and could signal in case an early rising farmer chose this time to use the road. Another girl was posted at the old church, as a safeguard against any blighter who may decide to shorten his circuit by turning earlier and thus gain a better timing.

Of a field of twelve cars that morning, only my Riley had a cubic capacity over 1000, so, apart from five seconds which we agreed should be added to my timing, we dispensed with handicapping and decided to run the thing on a free for all basis, the fastest car over two runs to be the outright winner. To increase the size of the field, a few of us arranged to swop cars and to essay two runs with our own and two with the other, Bill and I amongst them.

Apart from an exhaust system which parted company with its Austin Seven Swallow, and another Seven which began to exhaust through its cylinder-head gasket, all went well with our climb during the first half of the programme. The burnt oil vapour which slowly diluted itself in the early morning ground mist, and the busy notes of the exhausts combined to produce a very satisfactory effect. Bill Stewart and I began to congratulate ourselves on having another successful event to our credit, and then came my turn at the wheel of Bill's Midget. As I was as proud of this little gem as was its owner, it is perhaps right that we should take a backward glance at this, the first of the famous Midgets, before I go on to describe what happened when I drove one in Martindale.

## 'Auto'-Biography

Cecil Kimber of MGs brought two new cars to the 1928 Motor Show at Olympia. One was the MG Six 18/80, a 2½-litre open four-seater with overhead camshaft, and capable of some 80 m.p.h. Retailing as it did at £525, it was a car to be viewed with envy by we impecunious types. The other was the M-type Midget, of which Bill's was an example of the first few models off the line, that is to say it had a fabric body, whereas later models were to be metal-clad. Its top speed, provided by the 847 c.c. engine – also overhead camshaft – was claimed to be in the region of 60 m.p.h., and the car sold at a modest £175, a price which brought sports car ownership within the reach of more and more people, who had hitherto had to be content with more mundane cars with no pretensions to performance. Of the two cars the little Midget was by far the better looking, its 'cobby', sporty look, boat-shaped tail, cycle-type wings and wire wheels combining to assure it an instant success. Simple in design to the point of starkness, it was the forerunner of the long line of Midgets which was to follow, and the M-type was in fact the basis of the 750 c.c. car EX 120, with which George Eyston achieved 103·13 m.p.h. at Montlhery in 1931.

As, at the drop of the flag and the click of the stopwatch, I commenced my climb in the MG that morning, I was, for Bill's sake, anxious to put up a good show and return a fast time, and, as I came out of bottom gear at the summit and changed up to begin the sprint down to the church, I was aware that my time was in fact fast at that stage. A rapid turning manœuvre at the church, a quick wave to Jill Stanton who stood leaning against the old porchway, and we were away again back up the less severe side of the hill.

I had been aware of sheep beginning to wander nearer and nearer to the road on my previous climbs, and had a moment's anxiety when one of them almost stepped into my path, but so far they had not created any hazard. This time, however, as I reached the summit again, there was no mistaking the intentions of one which was indubitably a ram, and which stood firmly in the centre of the road, head lowered and horns positively quivering with rage.

15. 'At times a contrived drift is successfully accomplished.' Cornering at Southport

16. On the banking at Brooklands

17. To me it looked appalling, but it started 'on the button'. The Morris 'Bullnose'

18. The Riley 'Monaco' of happy memory, 1927

*Roman orgy*

Obviously its patience was exhausted, and it was probably thinking that if it allowed this nonsense to go on 'There'll never be another ewe!'

We did not meet head on. I executed a rapid avoiding action – but he made his point nonetheless. He took a side-swipe at the car as I passed him, and I cringed in my seat as I heard the unmistakable sound of tearing fabric. Back at the foot of the hill I leapt out of the car and stared in dismay at the damage. The ram's horn had ripped the entire length of the car door and the fabric gaped open to reveal the timber framing. Bill, to his eternal credit, after I had explained and he had inspected, grinned and said, 'What the hell! We'll fix it.'

Before continuing with our programme, we sent a team up the fell to clear the road of sheep, and the ram was discovered undamaged and contentedly grazing, honour being satisfied. Then came the turn of Tommy Benson in the Swallow which had lost its exhaust pipe. Making a din which was astonishing considering the diminutive size of its engine, he threw the little Austin up the hill and vanished around the second hairpin. Suddenly the din stopped abruptly and there was a metallic crunching sound. The girl on Hollin Fell waved frantically at us and started to run down towards the road. Four of us jumped into the Riley and we sped up the hill, to find the Austin apparently deeply embedded in the fell side, and Tommy slouched over his wheel, blood streaming from his forehead.

Fortunately the girl whose wave had alerted us was a nursing sister with skills all her own, and, after sizing up the situation with complete calmness – setting us all an example – she instructed us how to lift Tommy from the car and to lay him on the grass, where she tended to his wound, an unpleasant gash above his left eye. I remember his look of utter bewilderment as he asked, 'What the hell happened then?'

The only way to answer his query was to examine the car, and it soon provided the answer. The off-side track-rod end had left its mate; no sign of any nut nor any trace of there having been a split-pin. Obviously bad maintenance on Tommy's part, but this was not the time to rub that in. The thing to do was to get him to the nearest hospital, for the gash needed stitches. And, taped up from the resources of a first-aid kit, he was sent off in a member's car and accompanied by our nursing friend, to Penrith, whilst Bill and I and a few others set about the problem of putting the Swallow back into a driveable condition. A spare nut and a bent nail from a tool-kit cured the steering; the spare wheel was fitted to replace the one buckled by the crash, and all was well.

We were all somewhat shaken, this being the first accident we had suffered in any of our events, and the rest of the programme was called off. There was no shortage of drivers and thus no problem of getting the Swallow back home again, so we all returned, not a little chastened.

Tommy bears his 'Martindale' scar to this day, but the Midget, two weeks after its brush with the ram, fared much better. A visit to our friends, the boatmen of the Southport Marine Lake, produced a length of old sail-cloth, which, applied to the car door with surgical skill and followed by a complete re-painting of the car, by brush, and in a vivid red, left it looking like new again.

# CHAPTER EIGHT

## *A pair of swallows*

Perhaps the run-down of the business, after a year or two of success, was in no small measure due to my neglect of the duties allocated to me. After the first year, when I had a real enthusiasm for the shop, I was to find that motoring had me in such a grip, that my interest in the job for which I was being quite well paid, rapidly diminished. I took more and more time off, leaving all such matters as the administration to father, and the over the counter retail work to the small staff we employed. And if the Riley had been less reliable and had caused me to dip my hand in my pocket for frequent repairs, I would not have been so keen to drive farther and farther afield. But the little Monaco never once let me down, nor in fact did Bill Stewart's Midget ever give him cause for concern, and, sharing the two cars alternately we began to think nothing of running south to watch a Brooklands meeting, motoring through the night on a Friday and returning on the Sunday. If there was a rally or a scramble in Yorkshire we would go along to watch or to participate. If Shelsley Walsh promised an unusual or exciting programme, we would be there.

That paragons exist I am well aware. I fear I was not of their number, and I like to think – perhaps to salve an uneasy conscience – that most of us in our middle teens, of whatever generation we belong, tend to regard the world as owing us a living, and certainly take advantage of parents who are less than strict.

There came a time of course when even I began to realize that our business was taking a downward course; that certain customers were leaving us and that those who remained were spending less and less. There were no recriminations pointed in my direction from father, and we decided that the conditions which prevailed during those years – years of unemployment and little spending power – were the factors behind our reduced income, and that the cut-price shops which were opening in the town were another factor.

When a decision was reached that the Riley had to go, I gulped, although, after studying our falling sales graph, I fully appreciated that capital had to be recovered from certain sources, of which the car was one. So, after cash was pumped into the business from the sale of the car, sundry sales and a minor 'other interest', nemesis seemed to be fended off.

Then came a period when a series of cars passed through my hands, some good, some bad, but mostly indifferent, and none of them cost more than £15! Most of them should remain decently interred in the past, merely painful memories, like the one which was found to have sawdust in its sump and back axle. Yes – perfectly true, and I was the one to fall for it. Or the one which had wooden wedges driven beneath its front suspension U-bolt clamps; wedges which I removed in disgust only to hammer them back in again when the car developed a violent wheel wobble without them. Or the one which regularly deposited its sump oil on the garage floor each night, and defied all efforts to discover the cause. Yes – that is true too. There was something decidedly creepy about that one – a car which cried out to be the subject of exorcism, a car with a devil all its own.

A few of the cars which came my way are worthy of friendly mention, one in particular figuring in an incident which puzzles me to this day, and which perhaps some student of erotica or a reader with a Freudian bent can explain away.

The car was a much battered 1927 Jowett 'Seven', a ghastly-looking four-door saloon which originally sold at £185, and which we bought from a local barber for £12 10s (The number of cars we seemed to buy from that barber. I am sure he 'trimmed' us in more ways than one). Of the car itself I remember it had a 907 c.c. flat-twin engine with astonishing pulling power; Delco coil

## A pair of swallows

ignition and, I think a Cox-Atmos carburettor. Of the true sit-up-and-beg variety it had a flimsy, brush-painted body with nickel plated radiator, and its cheap and nasty artillery-type wheels gave it a strangely insecure, unsolid look, A queer 'phut-phut-phutting' noise emanated from its exhaust and, although the subject of much hilarity at the car club meets, it could out-climb most of the Austin Sevens.

Having no garage of our own at the time, I housed the car in a disused shed belonging to a neighbouring milkman, and one winter's evening I had to dash across the road to fetch it, in order to take my old dog, Jack, to the vet. Reaching the shed and flinging the doors open took seconds only, and as I began to climb aboard the car there was a feminine shriek, a muffled mutter, a flurry, and two people shot out of the car and dashed away across the yard. Damned annoyed at the liberty taken, I switched on the headlights, illuminating the rapidly retreating couple, and then sat for a while, completely baffled. For in the light I recognized the backs of a married couple, who lived a mere few doors away from the dairy. That I had disturbed them in 'affairs marital' became immediately obvious when I found a frilly garment lying across the back of the front passenger seat.

Explain that to me if you can. Why, in someone else's car, with their own home only two hundred yards away . . . ? I bought a padlock for the shed doors the next day. After all, if anyone was going to use that back seat . . . !

I have heard the theory about a fast-moving car having an aphrodisiac effect on certain people. But does an elderly Jowett, static and in a shed, have the same effect?

Another Hotchkiss-engined Bullnose followed the Jowett, this time a saloon. Costing us £10, it was what the trade are pleased to describe as 'a good runner'. Apart from its looks, which I still despised, I could not fault it, especially as Bunny and I were now becoming inseparable in our free time, and the Morris became our courting car. Amongst the club members it became known as 'The Office' for the simple reason that, at our various events, it

## 'Auto'-Biography

performed just that function, being quite hopeless as a sporting carriage. I was in fact beginning to despair of ever being able to enter a car of my own in any future event, a feeling which the next car did nothing to dispel, although it did provide me with a damned good meal at a time when I needed one.

This was a Singer, of indeterminate age and of which memories are vague. I know it was a tourer with the usual discoloured mica side curtains, and I think it was powered by an engine aspiring to 10 h.p. I do recall that it had no guts, and that its suspension was rock-like.

I had, somewhat rashly, agreed to take Bunny and her aunt to Hounslow where they were to take a holiday, and I also agreed to take an elderly friend of the aunt home to Banbury en route for the south. The friend was taking home with her, as a special treat for her relatives, one of the specialities of the house of Madge Brewer, a confectioner noted in Southport for the quality of her pies and *gâteaux*. This was a huge pork pie, sufficient for six people; one of those delectable beauties surmounted by a decorated crust on which rested a succulent jelly, and a pie within which nestled a hard-boiled egg.

For the entire length of the journey from Southport to Banbury, the friend sat bolt-upright in the back seat, nursing in its paper bag the pie from which she refused to be parted. We reached Banbury safely, deposited her at her home, and pressed on to London, where I left my passengers and set off on my return journey. Thinking to complete the run overnight, I reckoned without a torrential downpour which proved my lighting to be quite inadequate, and compelled me to sleep in the car until daylight. When I awoke and for some reason glanced into the back of the car, there was the pie in its paper bag, down on the floor where its owner must have placed it temporarily as she left the car.

The sporting thing would have been to deliver the pie to Banbury, no great distance from the spot where I had slept, and, to my credit I did toy with the idea. However, the rumblings of an empty stomach completely wiped out any chivalrous notions,

## A pair of swallows

and the pie was eaten, in three sittings, on the way home. Never did pork pie taste quite so good.

Then came the kind of luck which one tends to chalk up amongst the red letter occasions in life. Some few days after returning from the London trip I delivered, in the Singer, the weekly order to the home of father's friend Teddy. As I left the house, I found him staring at the Singer, muttering to himself and prodding it in sundry places with a stubby finger.

'What in God's name is this?' he asked.

I explained as best I could that the present financial state of the business only justified such a car, and I rushed to the defence of the old Singer, telling him it had just completed a run to London and back.

'Don't care if it took you to Timbuctoo and back. That's just pure luck and this car's damned bad economy. You'll spend more on repairs than the thing is worth. Get rid of it!' And, as I started to drive away he called out, 'Tell your father to come and see me!'

Father did go to see him, on foot, and returned by car. When I returned home from the club that evening, he told me that the Singer would have to stand out all night, that the garage was occupied. Knowing that the Singer objected to such treatment and retaliated by being difficult to start in the morning, I was annoyed and walked across to see if I could make room in the stable, thinking that father had stored some cases of canned goods there.

There were no canned goods. The stable was occupied by Teddy's Austin Seven Swallow, gleaming in the light of my torch; immaculate as Teddy's cars always were. I guessed wrongly in supposing that the car had been lent to father until the Singer could be replaced. The Swallow was its replacement. Teddy had sold it to father for £15, and its speedometer registered a mere 19,000 miles!

This Swallow became the first car I was to own, in my own name, and paid for with my own money. I scraped up the £15 from my savings, and never was money better spent.

*'Auto'-Biography*

The chassis on which the smart Swallow coachwork was built was pure Austin Seven, and the car retained all the endearing features and irritating – at times infuriating – tricks of the Seven. It had a 747 c.c. water-cooled, side-valve, four-cylinder engine, transmission being through a single-plate clutch, three-speed gearbox and thence via a divided propeller shaft, the rear half of which was enclosed in a torque tube. The frame of the chassis formed an A to the ends of which were bolted the quarter elliptic rear springs. Springing at the front was achieved by transverse leaf springs, shackled at either end, the axle being located by diagonal radius arms. The general geometry of the suspension had the effect of keeping the driver very much on the alert, the car having a queer habit of 'steering from the back'.

The car could boast four-wheel brakes, but, the rear shoes being activated by the foot pedal and the front by a hand lever, anyone effecting a smooth and parallel stop, without locking either front or rear shoes to their drums, was a good driver indeed.

The free clutch travel amounted to about half-an-inch, with the result that if one were careless in starting off, the car would jerk embarrassingly away, and I have seen many a haughty look wiped from an owner's face when this happened.

For all its faults, the Seven endeared itself to a large number of people by virtue of its longevity, utter reliability and cheapness of running. And when William Lyons and William Walmsley, of the Swallow Sidecar and Coachbuilding Company – which operated from a back street in Blackpool – graced the little Seven with one of their bodies, the Austin suddenly grew up, taking its place amongst the contemporary MGs and Rileys. The Swallow treatment was also applied to such cars as Wolseley, Swift and Standard with the same successful results. We were not to know at the time that, from the swept-winged, low-roofed look of the Swallow bodies, the styling features of the famous line of Jaguars which followed were already beginning to emerge.

The example which came my way was indeed 'as new; one careful owner', and although, regrettably, it was to stay with me

*A pair of swallows*

for all too short a time, I was as proud of that car as I have been of any since. From the roof to the high waistline, and on two-thirds of its bonnet, it was painted in a deep blue, the rest of the car being cream. Mounted on the scuttle just forward of the V-shaped windscreen were two cowl-shaped ventilators, but I cannot recall if they were merely decorative or if indeed they did function. The roof protruded beyond the screen, giving a peaked cap effect, and, with the silver painted wire wheels surmounted by the swept wings, the total effect was, aesthetically, good.

The Singer was disposed of, to our friend the barber, for £7 10s and, within a week, he had sold it again for £11. That man was in just the right kind of business. Not many motor dealers can pin their customers down in a chair, tie them down with a bib, and wield a cut-throat razor while they sing the praises of a car.

If my brother Tommy has not figured too largely in my narrative it is due I think to the fact that our interests differed so much, and there was a disparity in our ages of about five years. Matters motoring absorbed most of my spare time, whereas he was keen on his cricket and rugby. However, Tommy certainly fell for the Swallow, and had it not been for the fact that I could honestly claim the car to be mine, and could thus dictate as to who should drive it, I am sure I should have lost it to him at the weekends.

By the time the Austin came into my hands, he had left Leyland's publicity office and taken a similar job, on increased pay, with Hans Renold, the chain people. One Friday, less from a feeling of brotherly affection than for the sheer pleasure of driving to Manchester, I went to collect him at the factory, to bring him home. Generously I allowed him to take the wheel and, as we were passing one of the used car lots which seemed to exist on every street corner of the city suburbs, I spotted another Swallow parked amongst a collection of four-wheeled bric-à-brac, and wearing on its windscreen the price tag – £25.

'Whoah! Hold it, Tommy!'
'What's troubling you?'
'Pull in and come look at this.'

## 'Auto'-Biography

Obviously this Swallow had not led a pampered life with its previous owner or owners; its paintwork, green and cream, was dull and fading, and its seating shabby. Mechanically however it seemed sound enough, and, after a test run around the district – my own car held as security by the shirt-sleeved 'sales manager' – I suggested to Tommy that he make an offer for it, that he should dig into his pocket for once and buy a car of his own.

The suggestion took him so much by surprise that, within five minutes, a deal was effected, and in exchange for £20 he found himself the owner of an Austin Seven Swallow and a tank full of petrol. I believe I was so astonished and Tommy so bemused, that neither of us noticed that the car was untaxed and uninsured. Nor did realization dawn until the following morning when we both went into town in his car and parked it outside the people's emporium, Marks and Spencers.

Leaving the store bearing a tin of aluminium paint with which I intended to brighten up the wire wheels of Tommy's acquisition, we found, standing beside the car, the largest policeman I had ever seen in my life.

'This yours?' he asked.

'Er – yes.'

He stabbed an enormous finger at the windscreen.

'Where's the tax?'

We both stared at the screen, devoid of any tax disc, and then at each other.

'Oh lumme,' we muttered simultaneously.

'Insurance?'

Dumbly, we shook our heads.

'Driving licence?'

At this we both beamed and produced our licences, which he proceeded to study meticulously, the little stiff-backed covers looking like postage stamps in his huge fists. He handed them back and, extracting a black book from his breast pocket, and using the car's roof as support, he scribbled industriously before tearing a page out and handing it to me. It was unmistakably a 'ticket' and,

*A pair of swallows*

as if it were red hot, I thrust it at Tommy, who was trying hard to look completely unconcerned in the midst of the grinning onlookers in Southport's busiest shopping street.

'Now, you can't drive that until you get it insured and taxed. You'll have to tow it away.'

Feeling extremely small, we agreed that Tommy should stay with the car and that I should hop a 'bus home, returning with my car and a length of rope. Before rushing back to Tommy's assistance I told father, briefly, what had happened.

'Now wait – hold your horses. Who gave you the ticket?'

I described the enormous chap in blue, and father grinned.

'Right – I'll come back with you.'

Returning to the scene of our crime, I parked as close to Tommy's car as space permitted. Out 'bobby' was now standing on the other side of the road, his huge bulk seeming to fill the entrance to the railway station behind him. Father waved and beckoned and the giant, grinning in recognition, waded through the traffic.

'Morning, Ernie.'

'Morning, Bill,' and, showing him the ticket, 'Can you do anything about this?'

The law stared hard at Tommy and then at me.

'These your boys, Ernie? Well, why didn't they say so?' and, without more ado he reached for the flimsy paper and tore it up.

As we returned home, towing a Swallow with a Swallow, father explained that the constable was one of his old Vulcan men, and that when I described his size, he knew at once who it would be. How that policeman explained away to his sergeant the carbon copy of that ticket, I shall never know. Or perhaps the sergeant also once worked for father. But I mentally praised father's widespread influence and have held the gentlemen of the police in very high esteem ever since, especially large ones.

Tommy never did develop an affection for that car; he did not keep it long enough. He seemed to think I was responsible for

*'Auto'-Biography*

his expenditure of £20, which, as his girl friend repeatedly reminded him, would have have been better put aside for their forthcoming marriage. Well, if I was responsible, then at least I made him a profit, in selling the car for £25 to Jack Ayrton, a fellow club member, who was to use it to great effect in our various events. Unfortunately it was to be written off in an extraordinary way at the end of a day which started with great promise.

The occasion was the Shelsley Walsh meeting of May 27, 1933, a meeting Bill Stewart and I planned to watch as soon as we read the list of entrants in the previous week's *Motor*. Earlier that year MGs had brought out a new car, called it the 'Magnette' and with it jumped straight into the world's motoring headlines, taking both the team prize and a class win in the Italian Mille Miglia. The driving teams in the 1000-mile race had been Sir Henry Birkin and Bernard Rubin, Earl Howe and H. C. Hamilton, and George Eyston with Count 'Johnny' Lurani.

When therefore, we read that two of the actual cars which had competed in Italy were to appear at Shelsley, one in the hands of Count 'Johnny' himself and the other driven by Miss Fay Taylour – the motor-cycle speedway rider – we were quite determined to be there.

Jack Ayrton, hearing us discussing our plans, asked if he could join us, and we arranged that each of us should take his girl along and motor to Worcestershire in convoy, leaving late on Friday and travelling through the night. And Jack produced a trump card which pleased us all, in telling us he had a cousin who would be with the BBC outside broadcast team, and who would no doubt arrange for us to have a good vantage point.

And so it proved, for when we eventually reached Shelsley, stowed our cars away in one of the fields, and Jack enquired at the BBC caravan, parked near the start, as to the whereabouts of his cousin, we were told to climb up to the S-bends and to look for him there. Made welcome at the OB hut we were able to stand within a wattle-fenced enclosure from which we had a splendid view of the approach and of the S-bend itself. We were also able

*A pair of swallows*

to listen to Major Vernon Brook painting – through his microphone – vivid word pictures of the cars in action, and describing the scene not only to the usual 'domestic' listening audience, but to many more thousands over the Empire network; a new innovation. And when to those countless listeners one added the 15,000 or more spectators who turned up at the hill that day, one would have expected Shelsley to put up a good show.

But although the cars were there, and the 'big names', the weather was to win the day. Skies heavy with cloud produced a steady miserable drizzle throughout the meeting, making the surface of the hill greasy and treacherous which resulted in times being slower than had been hoped for.

The cars we had really come to watch, the Mille Miglia Magnettes, were, relatively, slow, neither of them figuring in the awards list at the end of the day. I recall George Eyston, in Fay Taylour's car, clocking 51·8 seconds after she, in the same car, had recorded 54·4. And Count 'Johnny' Lurani either found his Magnette out of form, or he was unhappy with a strange hill in appalling weather, for his best time was 57 seconds. E. R. Hall, driving his own privately entered Magnette, was to beat both the Mille Miglia cars with a time of 48 seconds.

It fell to John Bolster in his JAP motor-cycle-engined special – which was to acquire, in multi-engined form, the name 'Bloody Mary' – to provide the greatest excitement of the day. Sitting far back at the end of a chassis constructed mostly of wood, and lifting his right elbow high to avoid the tyre-tread, he came up the hill towards our vantage point, exhaust screaming and suggesting a fast time, when, just at the approach to the first curve of the 'S' his car skidded. Bolster corrected rapidly only to skid off on the other tack, and the car rolled. For ghastly seconds, and for several yards, he seemed to bear the full weight of the car on his bare head, and it seemed inevitable that he would be killed.

The car tipped over again, back on to its wheels and Bolster sat, hands to his head, blood seeping though his fingers. Miraculously his injuries, though bad enough, were not as severe as we had

## 'Auto'-Biography

feared, and when, these days, I see and hear him in the pits at race meetings, with hirsute face and wearing his deerstalker, remarking gleefully that 'Rindt has retired with broken suspension', or 'Hill is in with loss of oil pressure', I marvel as I look back at that day in 1933.

As I write, the following results of that spring Shelsley are on my desk.

| | | |
|---|---|---|
| 750 c.c. | Racing – A. N. Maclachlan (Austin) | 50·8 seconds |
| | Sports – R. F. Turner (Austin) | 52·0 seconds |
| 1100 c.c. | Racing – E. R. Hall (MG Magnette) | 48·0 seconds |
| | Sports – E. R. Hall (MG Magnette) | |
| 1500 c.c. | Racing – R. G. Nash (Special) | 45·6 seconds |
| | Sports – R. T. Grogan (Frazer-Nash) | 49·4 seconds |
| 2-litres | Racing – N. A. Carr (Bugatti) | 46·0 seconds |
| | Sports – C. M. Needham (Frazer-Nash) | 54·2 seconds |
| 3-litres | Raymond Mays (Villiers) | 44·8 seconds |
| | Sports – L. Bachelier (Bugatti) | 51·8 seconds |
| 4½-litres | Racing – Count Premoli (Maserati-Bugatti) | 47·2 seconds |

*A pair of swallows*

   Sports – J. W. Whalley  54·4 seconds
     (Ford)

Over 4½ Racing – No entrants
   Sports – H. H. Stisted  53·4 seconds
     (Mercedes)

 We had planned to dine that evening at The Swan Hotel, Tenbury Wells, which was the Mecca for competitors and enthusiasts of Shelsley, hoping to rub shoulders with such drivers as Mays and Eyston. But, as soon as we saw the packed car park and crowded bar, we realized we should be lucky if we secured even a sandwich, and pressed on to another pub farther north, where we dined well and I scribbled notes for a newspaper article on the meeting.

 The pub we chose was somewhat off the route Bill and I normally used on our trips to Shelsley, but Jack assured us that he knew the way to the main road north, and started up his engine ready to lead our convoy.

 We each bleeped our horns as a signal to get under way, and Jack slipped his Swallow's tricky clutch. None of us spotted the huge Humber which bore down on Jack's car as he left the pub yard to join the main road. Suddenly it was there, had side-swiped the Swallow and pushed it hard against a stone gate-post. There was no high speed involved, it was just a case of a heavy weight clouting a lesser one. But the result was astonishing, both sides of the Swallow being crushed, the car being sandwiched between Humber and gate-post.

 We wrenched at the driving door, but the handle left its moorings and it took a heavy tyre lever to get the thing open. Jack and his girl friend Ann, shaken but apparently unhurt, crawled out, and we all stood surveying the damage. It was at once obvious that no amount of panel-beating could possibly restore the original shape to the Swallow, yet the only damage to the Humber was a scraped front wing and a rumpled running board.

*'Auto'-Biography*

Names were exchanged and insurance companies noted, the Swallow was pushed to one side of the yard, and Jack and Ann, after a rest in the pub's lounge, joined Bunny and me for the return home. We were all very subdued, and I wished that when I had passed that used car lot with Tommy, only a few weeks ago, I had kept my big mouth shut.

And it seemed that this episode in some way signalled the end of a very pleasant era. Gradually our club membership dwindled as people left, to become doctors, solicitors, or joined their fathers' various businesses in Liverpool and Manchester. Attempts by Bill and me, the diehards of the club, to stir up interest in further events, seemed to meet with apathy, resistance and a general lack of keenness. It was all very sad. We were growing up and there were careers to be made.

Even I, in due course, realized that I too had a career to think about. A family committee meeting reached the unanimous decision that the business should be sold, while it was still worth more than had been paid for it. This decision reached, I took a temporary job as a traveller for one of the wholesale firms which had supplied the shop. Temporary, because I was going through an indecisive period, uncertain if the food trade held the key to the future, or whether I should follow my leanings towards engineering design and production. On the one hand, a career in sales with one of the major food manufacturers promised a life of travel and much driving. On the other, the smell of the machine-shop and the foundry had been in my nostrils since childhood, and, after all, the Knowles family had always been engineers.

19. Stark, slow, but trend-setting. The first 'Midget', MG M8-type, 1928

20. Jaguar in embryo? 'The Austin Seven "Swallow"'

21. I drove it around Brooklands, and nearly owned it. The MG J3-type 'Midget', 1933

22. Perhaps the best looker of the line. I sold many of these. The MG TF-type 'Midget' of 1953

CHAPTER NINE

# The 'Tiger', the Bentley and the J.3

'Blast those cobbles, and blast that drip-feed.' So saying, I picked myself up from the roadway, felt around for broken bones, and answered the anxious call, 'Are you all reet?' from the farmer who had dashed to his door on hearing the clatter of the Triumph as it met the ground.

'That's the third time this week,' he said as he helped me lift the bike from the road.

'It's the fourth,' I replied, 'and it's becoming a bad habit.'

Almost overnight, it seemed, my world had changed. The shop had changed hands; we had a new home in a Southport suburb; father had joined a friend with a factory in Salford making accessories for textile machinery, and I was now learning to be an engineer, working in the very factory, outside Bolton, which he had left so many years before.

I commuted daily, after a miserable few months of being in digs, leaving home at six in the morning and returning around eight in the evening. My transport was a Triumph 'Tiger' 250 c.c. trials bike, a handsome and satisfyingly fast beast, with upswept 'pipe' and from which I had, for the fourth time in a week, and at the very same spot, just parted company.

I knew conditions which, when combined, always produced this severance of self from saddle, but it seemed I had still not learned my lesson. If you have a rainy evening, a greasy cobbled road, an oil drip-feed lubricating a primary chain too generously, and splashing on to the side of a rubber tyre, and if, given all these

## 'Auto'-Biography

ingredients you lean your bike at too acute an angle when cornering on the cobbles, you have the ideal recipe for a crunch.

Fortunately the radius of the corner prevented high speed, and my heavy rain-sodden leather coat absorbed most of the shock, so I escaped personal damage. And usually, apart from a bent clutch handle and a scraped front mud-guard, the well built machine suffered little from such ill-treatment. This time, however, the bike looked different when we picked it up. The handlebars were at forty-five degrees to the front wheel and, although I held the wheel tightly between my legs and heaved, those handlebars positively refused to budge. Like a fool I had left my tool-kit in the garage at home, and the friendly farmer could only muster a huge wrench, immovable with rust.

What then, with a girl waiting at home and a date with a Mayoral Ball, does one do? There was only one answer – ride the damned thing home. And so I did, right arm stretched far forward and left tucked into my hip, trying to look completely unaware of the ribald remarks issuing from passing vehicles.

'You've put that lot together badly, mate.'

'Make your ruddy mind up – you can't go both ways.'

Ultimately I solved the problem. There were two ways home from Bolton, one through Chorley and Rufford, a good fast road, and the other over Parbold Hill, three miles the shorter, but which took in the cobbled bit. The answer then was to use the Chorley route on a wet day, and the more scenic Parbold run when dry. But I never did cure that drip-feed, nor did I ever seem able to afford a new, oil-free tyre.

My decision to go into engineering was not lightly made. The trade was struggling through a period of depression, alleviated to some extent by War Department orders, which were perhaps some small sign of recognition that in Italy there existed a large-chinned buffoon and in Germany a sinister character with a tiny moustache.

Certainly there were no high wages or salaries being paid, and one had to be something of an optimist to enter a trade which seemed, to say the least, 'dicey'. However, when an uncle who was 'top brass' at Dobson and Barlows, offered to have me trained in machine shop practice at their Bradley Fold factory, I took the opportunity, despite the distance involved, and in the belief that with one uncle in the top echelon, another a departmental head and sundry cousins who were either on the staff or foremen, I should have a comprehensive training and not be confined to one branch of the trade.

Realizing that I could now no longer afford the running costs, I sold the Swallow to a good home, with the blessing of that generous sportsman Teddy, and I parted from it with great regret. At about the same time, Bill Stewart and I also parted company, he moving south to take up a surveying job – luckier than I in being able to retain his faithful Midget. We spent an evening crying into our beer – and we never met again. My erstwhile motoring chum was to be killed at Dunkirk.

My time at Dobson's was marked by a few memorable events, but it taught me, I fear, little of the engineering I had come to learn. I found that, suddenly, I had too many friends. The news that I was 'Ernie's' son and 'Arthur's' nephew went through the factory as if by bush telegraph, and, no matter if I were tending a mechanical hack-saw, cutting steel rod, feeding a screw-threader with components to be tapped, or merely scraping burrs from finished components, I would soon have three or four of the older hands around me, recalling the Bolton of long ago, the Bolton of the cotton boom, when Dobson's made looms for the mills of the world, and when some of these chaps went out to Russia to teach 'them Ruskis' how to run them.

Even amongst the younger employees there was never any suggestion that my being there smacked of nepotism. The fact that I was a Knowles seemed adequate reason for my presence at Dobson's, and, with one notable exception, they all accepted me. It seemed to me that our family name and those of Dobson and Barlow were synonymous.

I spent so much time chatting in the various shops that, no doubt after a discussion between uncle and the cousin who was my foreman, I was put in charge of a brand-new Herbert No. 4 turret lathe, probably in the hope that this would keep me so interested that there would be no time for chat. But even this ploy failed, people still gathered around my machine, staff and management included, and my work suffered.

But if I learned little of engineering, I did learn how to wield a cricket bat against some of the most devastating body-line bowling I have ever seen. For, every 'dinner-time' we played cricket on a field at the back of the factory, and those Boltonians certainly knew their cricket.

I remember one occasion vividly, in which the sole unfriendly type from the machine shop figured. Arnold was given to making snide remarks as I passed his machine, such as 'these bloody seaside snobs'. This annoyed me, as I certainly did not consider myself to be a bloody snob, nor any other kind of snob, and, whenever he was bowling during our cricket matches, I would take a delight in 'cracking him all over the field'. On this particular day, with my turn to take the bat came Arnold's turn with the ball, and he was obviously determined to stop the rot. He hurled the ball at me with venomous force, seeming to insert it into a slot which led, unerringly, to the knuckles of my left hand. Once – twice – he struck me, and I managed a sickly grin. But the third one was a beauty, made me drop the bat, writhe in anguish and give him best as he stood grinning at the other end.

As the afternoon wore on, my hand became swollen and stiff and I went to hold it under a cold water tap, passing a sneering Arnold on my way. When I returned, Charlie Turner, one of 'our team' on the cricket field, called out, 'All reet now, Artie?' and then 'Christ!' as he pulled his hand sharply from his lathe. As he held it up I could see that the middle finger was missing, down to the second knuckle. As he called to me he had trapped it between cutting tool and the component spinning in its chuck.

Sickened, I ran to his help, but he brushed me aside and groped around in the mixture of cutting fluid and turnings in the lathe well. He found the missing bit, wrapped it in a dirty rag which he

## The 'Tiger', the Bentley and the J.3

then proceeded to wrap around his hand. He walked calmly to my cousin's office, told him what happened, and, just as calmly, walked out of the machine shop. He then, by himself, took a bus to the hospital. Suddenly, my own damaged hand seemed nothing, nothing compared with what I had just seen.

Charlie returned to us in due course, *sans* finger. He had hoped that the severed piece could have been 'stuck on again', but he was disappointed. For the remaining months of my stay at the factory he continued to give us spirited renderings of 'Oley a rose', in a flat tenor voice which defeated the racket of the overhead shafting and belting, and he continued to assure us that the latest addition to his family was being fed on 'oyster milk'. And his accident had a salutary effect on me, in that I treated all moving machinery with the greatest respect from that time on.

Of all the memories of that period, those associated with the Triumph are the best. Ownership of a motor-bike was a very pleasant interlude in a lifetime spent amongst cars, an interlude which occurred at the right time, before the emergence of the postwar 'mods and rockers' made the mention of motor-cycles tantamount to using dirty words, and a time when such a machine was not frowned upon by other road users.

On a fine morning, when the mists were rising and before the rest of the country was awake, those runs to Bolton were a wonderful experience. With the roads to myself and on a perfectly tuned machine, I revelled in the rush of air, the high, crisp note of the exhaust, the snappy gear-changing with the foot pedal and the winding it up to sixty and seventy along the straights. And a gallon of petrol seemed to last indefinitely, and a gallon at a time was all I ever bought.

There were snags of course. On a wet morning things were not so good, and I would sigh for some genius to come up with a pair of goggles having an inbuilt screen-wiper. And then there was the irate neighbour who, in pyjamas and dressing gown, met me as I left our drive one morning.

'That contraption makes such a dreadful din when you start it, that it wakes the whole district. In future, walk the damned thing to the end of the road before you kick off.'

He had a point. Certainly, with one kick of the pedal and a quarter turn of the twist-grip, that Tiger started up with a wonderful snarl.

My old school-pal Rollo was going through his own motor-cycle phase at this time, riding a 350 c.c. BSA, and we took to visiting scrambles in various parts of the country. We also spent a summer holiday in the Isle of Man, taking the machines with us, and beating around the TT course early each morning, a time of day when the local gendarmerie frowned little if at all. As Rollo's 'Beesa' was a solid, standard road machine, with no pretensions to sportiness, and with a low-slung exhaust which prevented him from leaning at the corners, we took turns with the Tiger around the course, each trying to beat the time of the other. We really thought we were remarkably fast those mornings, until one day three professionals, practising, screamed past us and vanished into the distance in a haze of blue and aromatic smoke. We suddenly realized what rookies we were and gave it up for the rest of our stay.

At home, the Tiger also made itself useful at the Southport Motor Club beach meetings, the officials using me, instead of a telephone link, as a cheaper and less troublesome method of getting the mile sprint results to the control caravan. I would station myself at the end of the mile, memorize the cars' racing numbers as they flashed past the finish and then, giving the bike 'full bore' would dash back to control. I remember those officials ticking me off for giving the results to the gentlemen of the press before I entered the caravan. Protocol had arrived at the beach.

But my time at Dobson's was coming to an end. It was becoming increasingly obvious that I was wasting not only my own time but that of the chaps who were trying to teach me to be an engineer. I was in the wrong place, there being too many distractions, and – at least in my case – a complete absence of discipline, one factor which is essential in any workshop.

And, with the move from the Bolton factory, came the end of

## The 'Tiger', the Bentley and the J.3

my motor-cycling days. Before I parted with the Tiger, however, it figured in an incident which, in turn, led to a very moving experience.

Often, during my 'dry weather' runs home in the evenings, the runs via Parbold, I would overtake or be passed by another rider with an AJS machine. The initial competitive instinct to open up and to re-overtake, developed into a habit, and, whenever we met an exchange of grins would signal the start of a race, which would end at Kew Bridge, on the outskirts of Southport. Here, with a wave, we would separate, he turning left for the town while I pressed on to my own district.

On the Friday evening of my last week at Dobson's, I was riding home in somewhat subdued mood, sadness at saying goodbye to my Bolton friends conflicting with the knowledge that the move was necessary if I was to make any headway in engineering. Reaching the summit of Parbold and riding leisurely down to the plain below, I was passed by the AJS, its rider urging me on with a wave of his hand. As usual I accepted the challenge, and we had another exhilarating dice along the country roads, through Burscough village, on to Scarisbrick – where I mentally doffed a cap at my cobbled bit – and then on to the long straights which led to Southport.

I was leading as we approached Kew, and decided to wave him down; to explain that this would be the last of our races. For half an hour we chatted at the road-side and I found that he too was serving a premium apprenticeship with a Bolton engineering firm. When he told me that, in addition to the AJS he had an MG at home, I was so interested that he invited me to have a look at it the following morning.

Reaching his home on the Saturday, it seemed inevitable that his parents should know mine – everyone did in those days. Our fathers' paths had crossed frequently in the Vulcan era, and they were in fact brother free-masons of the same lodge. That his son Peter and I had never met previously was because I was schooled in Southport, and he, as a boarder, at Rossall.

## 'Auto'-Biography

If Bill Stewart's M-type had aroused my interest in MGs then Peter Shaw's 1933 J3 Midget established that interest very firmly. For those unfamiliar with the evolvement of these famous cars – and I suppose that is remotely possible – it should be briefly explained that the M-type stemmed from the popular, quantity-produced o.h.c. Morris Minor and, from the M – as I have said previously – came the record-breaking Montlhery EX 120. From this came the C-type racing car, of which only forty or so reached the public in production form. Clever shuffling of M and C components produced, first the J1s and J2s of 1932–33, and then the J3s of which Peter's was an example. (MG purists will demand strict accuracy in reminding me that, somewhere between the Cs and the Js was a D-type, but of this car – except that I believe it was a four-seater – memories are vague.)

The J was the first Midget to be designed in what came to be regarded as the classic MG shape, with long bonnet line, cutaway sided cockpit, slab tank, cycle-type wings and wire wheels. The 4 × 27 tyres as fitted to the M had been superseded by 4 × 19 on the J and the result was a very satisfactory low look. Of course it was a stark little car, devoid of all creature comforts, and of course one needed to be something of a contortionist to get into the thing, and something of a stoic to withstand its suspension. But, for its designers it was a major breakthrough and in direct contrast to the high, boxy look of its contemporaries. Unfortunately, although these new Midgets could be seen gleaming in the showrooms, one saw few on the roads, for not many in those days could afford the £175 which was 'list price'.

During several fast sprints up and down the beach that morning, sprints when we took the wheel alternately, I must have enthused so much about his car that Peter was prompted to come up with a bright idea. The following week he was going down to spend a holiday with an uncle near Weybridge, an uncle who had entree to Brooklands.

'Always something going on there,' he said. 'It's the International Trophy Race at the end of the week. Like to come with me?'

## The 'Tiger', the Bentley and the J.3

There was only one sensible answer to that, and I gave it. After the long working days at Dobson's, days made even longer with commuting on the bike, I was ready for a break before accepting a job I had been offered.

The same afternoon I took the Tiger to the showrooms of the local motor-bike 'king', Harry Brockbank. Harry jumped on to the saddle, drove the machine around a couple of blocks, and on his return counted out thirty-five one-pound notes into my hand. I gave him the 'log-book' and walked home. In the fourteen months which had elapsed since I bought the bike, I had lost just five pounds in depreciation. I had enjoyed my two-wheeled phase, had my fun, but was now looking forward to having a steering-wheel in my hands again.

Although, in the past few years, I had visited Brooklands on several occasions, it had always been as a spectator, paying entrance fees and confined to the enclosures. This time, it was different. Peter's Uncle Harry, owner of a large garage outside Weybridge, seemed to regard the racing circuit along the road as a mere extension of his own premises, and spent part of each working day out on the track, testing one car or another. Apparently he had acquired a reputation as a tuner of racing machines, and his services were in great demand by amateurs who, with a great variety of cars, were aspiring to make names for themselves at Brooklands. That we accompanied Uncle Harry on these daily forays went without saying, and we wallowed in the atmosphere of the famous track.

And, warned to keep well into the left-hand side of the circuit, and to keep off the bankings, Peter and I drove his MG around Brooklands for lap after lap. In some way, as if gathering inspiration and taking its cue from the new environment, the little 745 c.c. engine seemed to conjure up an extra knot or two, and, although we were overawed and completely outpaced by the heavier professional machinery which always seemed to be using the circuit, we were not at all unhappy to be there. We felt much as the true golfer feels when first setting foot on the hallowed turf of

*'Auto'-Biography*

St Andrews, slightly timorous, very respectful, and anxious to put up a good show.

That Uncle Harry must have been satisfied with the show we put up became obvious on the Wednesday morning of that week. Peter and I were browsing around the many workshops at the circuit, awaiting the arrival of his uncle, for we never took the MG out on to the track without his approval. When he did arrive he was at the wheel of a car we had seen tucked away in a corner of his garage, a car too hemmed in by others to permit of close inspection. It was one of the cars which the legendary 'W. O.' Bentley must have been drawing up during the 1914–18 war years, when he was occupied with the design of rotary aero-engines; the cars he introduced to the public late in 1921; the 3-litres, nobly proportioned and powered by 4-cylinder engines, and which were the forerunners of the famous Le Mans 'Red Labels'.

The engine of this early 3-litre had a bore of 80 mm. and a long stroke of 149 mm., which resulted in high torque at low revs. The head was non-detachable and the single overhead camshaft, which activated four valves to each cylinder, was driven by a vertical shaft at the front of the engine. Two magnetos supplied ignition to eight sparking plugs – two to each cylinder – and the engine had a compression ratio of only 4·3 to 1. Nevertheless this ratio provided 65 b.h.p. at 2500 r.p.m., sufficient to give the car a top speed of around 80 m.p.h. Suspension was by semi-elliptic springing and power was transmitted through a leather cone clutch.

Climbing into the passenger seat of the dark green 1922 example which Uncle Harry brought to Brooklands that day, was rather like climbing a library ladder to reach a rare volume. And to have opened that vestigial door would have been faintly ridiculous. One merely stepped over the threshold, so to speak, and then sat high, in a world of one's own.

The ride, although undoubtedly hard, was not harsh, and the bumps of that concrete track – so very noticeable in the MG – seemed to be ironed out as we motored around at about 70 m.p.h. At that speed the engine seemed to be merely ticking over, the

## The 'Tiger', the Bentley and the J.3

only noise being the rush of air above the high windscreen and the beautiful burble of the exhaust.

When Peter and I had each enjoyed two laps as passengers, Uncle Harry pulled in to the pit area and stepped out of the car.

'Well, who's first?' he asked, and Peter astonished me with his his reply.

'Not me,' he said, 'I'm not in this school,' and he strolled quietly away.

His uncle stared after him for a few moments and, as I took my seat at the wheel, murmured, 'Don't think young Pete's too well, you know.'

Driving that car was a revelation to me. The right-handed gear change moved through its gate like a knife through oily cheese, and although the clutch pedal seemed to have an abnormally long travel my changes were smooth, and the throttle response immediate. There was absolutely no free-play at the steering wheel and the car answered the helm without hesitation. I found I could place the car exactly where I wanted it and, although I never exceeded sixty, I did venture half-way up the Members' Banking and remember feeling mildly surprised that the angle did not seem to be as steep as I had expected. I remarked on this phenomenon to Uncle Harry who sat, arms folded, at my side.

'It's an illusion,' he said. 'It's steep enough, especially at the top – but the faster you are moving the shallower it seems.'

When, after I had covered three laps, we pulled into the pits, a Riley, seemingly in bare aluminium, pulled out in a hurry and shot away along the track.

'Freddie Dixon,' Uncle Harry shouted. 'Practising for Saturday.'

When we reached the MG it was quite obvious that Peter was off form. Sitting slumped at the wheel he looked pale and complained of a hell of a headache. I took him back to his aunt's house, and she called in a doctor who diagnosed a touch of sun. Well, for May it was certainly hot, so this verdict was accepted and Peter swallowed the placebos the doctor left for him.

On Saturday, May 6, 1935, we watched the International

## 'Auto'-Biography

Trophy Race run by the JCC. Peter seemed to be better and we both enjoyed the racing, and the unique pleasure of being in amongst it all at Brooklands, with complete freedom to wander where we wished. This was motor racing in its hey-day, and, for me, motor racing at its best.

There were type 59 3·3-litre Bugattis, driven by such as the Hon. Brian Lewis, Charles Martin and Lindsay Eccles; there were 2·3-litre Alfa-Romeo 'Monzas' – one of which had been hired for the meeting by a newcomer of whom few had heard, twenty-one-year-old Luis Fontes. There was Dr J. A. Benjafield driving a 2·6 Monza, a car previously owned by Fay Taylour, whom I had last seen at Shelsley. There were Freddie Dixon and Tommy Wisdom in Rileys (the latter sharing the driving with his wife Elsie, generally known as 'Bill'), E. R. Hall with his Magnette and Raymond Mays with a 2-litre ERA. These are the names I recall from an entry of thirty-seven starters, of whom only twelve finished the race.

The newcomer, Fontes, won the race in No. 13 – his hired Monza which he subsequently bought – and won it at a speed of 86·69 m.p.h. Second was Dixon's Riley, third Hall's Magnette, the Wisdoms' Riley was fourth and a B-type Alfa 'Monoposto' (single-seater) driven, I believe, by Richard Shuttleworth, was fifth.

It was a good day, but it was destined to be the last from which Peter Shaw derived any fun from life. Back home in Southport the following day, after a journey during which he refused to take the wheel of the MG, he was rushed by his own doctor into hospital. After two weeks of worry for his family and friends, a decision was reached that a serious brain operation was necessary, and, after the trepanning which the operation entailed, a stainless-steel plate was affixed to his skull.

Three weeks after his return home from hospital, and only two hours after I had visited him, to find him as I thought, well on the way to recovery, Peter died. And the steel plate, his father confided in me, had been a contributing factor in his death.

## The 'Tiger', the Bentley and the J.3

'I'm glad you and he spent that week together. Pete told me you both spoke the same language. But he loved everything to be absolutely normal, and could never have faced up to life wearing that damned thing.'

Quite soon after Pete's funeral, his parents asked me to dine with them one evening, and I was to receive another example of the generosity which seemed to be such a characteristic of so many of the friends I made in the pre-war years. And the offer made to me that evening was all the more extraordinary, in that it came from friends of only a few weeks' standing.

Mr and Mrs Shaw told me that the question of a future home for Peter's MG was bothering them. The motor-bike did not matter; Peter had merely regarded that as a cheap means of travel between his home and his job, and it could be disposed of to Harry Brockbank or one of the other dealers. But the car was a different matter; Peter had loved and cherished it, and they would like it to go to someone having the same feeling for the car.

'Arthur, we should like you to have it – as a gift. Just take it away tonight, and look after it.'

I drove the J3 home, reflecting on the strange sequence of events which had culminated in my owning a two-year-old MG, immaculate and recording a mere 11,000 miles on its speedometer. But my ownership was short-lived, and it took the wisdom of my father to make me relinquish the car.

'If you take the job you say you are taking, and if you are seen driving around the town in that, your life at work will be made intolerable.'

And of course he was right – he usually was. He had a chat with Mr Shaw, the car was returned, and a few days later I received a registered parcel in which I found Peter's Zeiss Ikon camera and a slip of paper bearing the one word 'Understood' and the signature 'John Shaw'.

CHAPTER TEN

# In which I change course

The place had changed, and the old atmosphere gone, to be replaced by something vaguely and undefinably unpleasant. The red-brick façade was the same, and the clock-tower marked once again the site of smoking foundries, humming machine shops and clattering assembly sheds. And beneath the tower, in those foundries and shops, worked a handful of the old Vulcan craftsmen and some of their sons. But the clock-tower no longer proudly wore the sign of 'Vulcan'; now the word 'Brockhouse' was emblazoned in red neon on its flanks, and, attracted by this announcement of the re-opening of the old factory, came a new breed of men, many of them decent, hard-working types who required nothing more than fair pay on a Friday in exchange for a week's work, and who mixed well with the old hands. But, amongst them came those who were merely on the make, and those who, before moving on again, came to stir up trouble. And it was these, the troublemakers, who seemed to have succeeded in changing the atmosphere of the old place.

When I learned that J. Brockhouse & Co, of West Bromwich, were taking the factory over for the production of tractors and trailers, and for the fulfilling of certain Government contracts, I saw an opportunity of following a chosen career, on my own doorstep as it were, and with a firm which promised much wider scope than had Dobson's. A chat with one of the directors of Brockhouse (Southport) Limited – a chat during which I confess to mentioning the name of Ernie Knowles – secured me an assurance that I could work my passage through the machine shop, the tool-room and the planning and drawing offices. What followed then, I was told, was up to me.

## In which I change course

I was thrown in at the deep end. Having advised my foreman on my first morning that I was a 'turner', accustomed to operating Herbert turret lathes, I was immediately allocated such a lathe. A box of rough castings and a blueprint were delivered to the lathe and I was told to get on with it. As I had never performed anything more ambitious at Bolton than the cutting of long lengths of tubing into smaller lengths, I was, to say the least, somewhat disturbed to discover that I was now expected to transform those shapeless castings into components having various diameters, of both the internal and external variety, and with most of the diameters threaded.

Fortunately, and thanks to father, I started reading blueprints at about the same time that I was introduced to Billy Bunter and the Greyfriars bunch, so I studied this one hoping to gain some clue as to what cutting tools I should need to set the machine up. As I pored over it, and made notes, an unsavoury-looking character sidled up to me.

'Got yer card, mate?'

'Er – pardon?'

'Got yer card– yer union card?'

Ah yes – I had been warned about this, and was able to produce a black card issued to me by the Bolton branch of the AEU. He looked disappointed when I handed it to him, but his face brightened considerably when he found himself able to say, 'Yer not paid up. Get bloody well paid up before tomorrow.'

This, it turned out, was the shop steward, and a pretty poor specimen of union official he turned out to be, full of his own imagined importance, and mouthing 'unionese' at every opportunity, punctuating it as do so many of his type, with swearing. There are many sincere examples of shop steward, who fulfil their functions well, whether one agrees with those functions or not. There are also many such as 'Willie', as I shall call him, automatically anti-management and ready at the slightest excuse to bring thousands of men out on strike over trivial grievances. But it is the men who vote the Willies into office, and I should have a much greater respect for unions if they cleared their ranks of this type.

Fortunately for me it transpired that I was a 'natural' with machine tools, and – until fate chipped in once more with a tempting offer which sent me off on another tack – I enjoyed my first stay at Brockhouse. I am afraid I joined one of the cliques with which the factory abounded, a group which, although not exactly anti-union, was most certainly anti-Willie, and took a frank delight in resisting his petty attempts to crack the whip and cause trouble. Because one of our number had a father on the Tory-controlled local council, we were, to Willie, all 'bloody young Tories', and on one occasion when we had aroused his wrath, he told us, 'You educated buggers have no right to be here. You should leave these jobs to them as needs 'em.'

Well, although our pay was abysmally low, it was certainly needed, especially by me. For it was high time I had another car.

The decision not to accept Peter's J3 was certainly the right one. Had I been seen around the town and driving to work in that immaculate little car, I should have been the target of Willie's vicious shafts of sarcasm, and of others of his ilk. But there was nothing to stop me from buying an old banger – for, judging by the examples which were dotted around the firm's car park each day, old bangers were accepted transport, for members of the proletariat.

I bought my car, from the operator of the lathe next to mine, who told me, mournfully, one morning, 'Got to sell it. Got to buy a bloody pram now.' On the Friday evening, having handed him the contents of my pay packet, plus two pounds seven shillings in cash, I drove my new acquisition – a 1928 Morris 'Minor' – home. The car was a four-seater (just), two-door saloon which, when new, had cost someone £125 and which had now cost me £5. This was the car from which had stemmed the Midgets, the original M-type having used a practically standard Minor overhead-camshaft power unit, and basically the same chassis.

Many of the reasons for the success and longevity of the Midgets

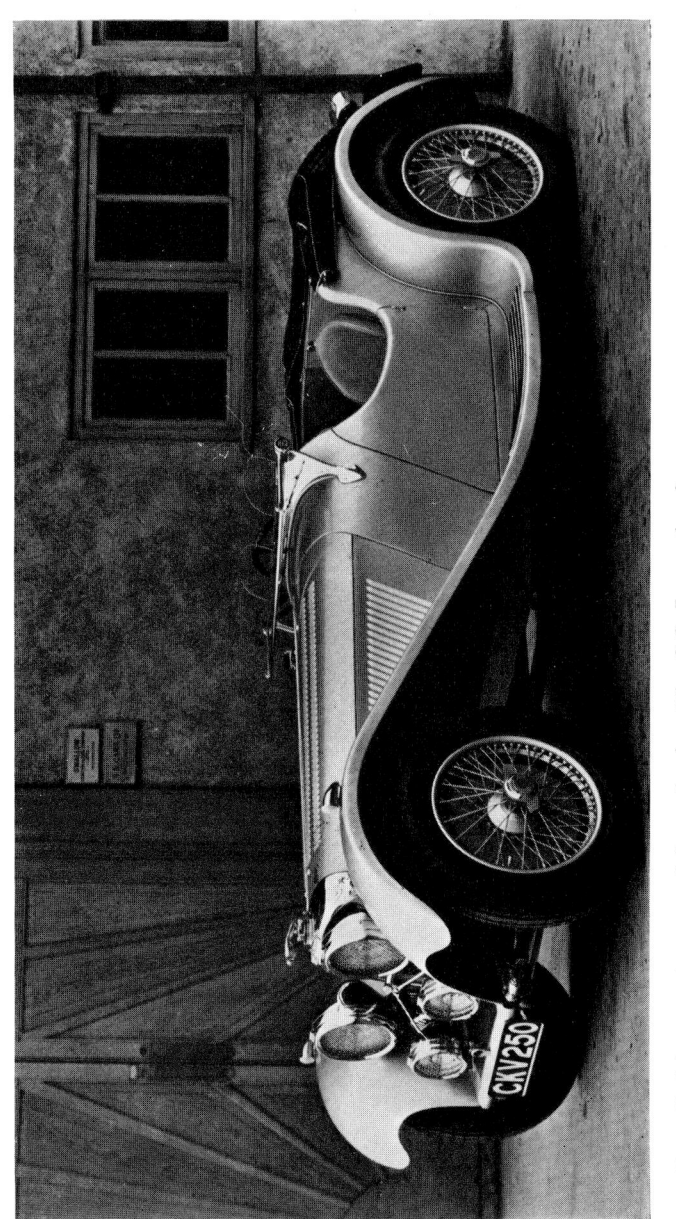

23. I revelled in restoring one of these classics. The S.S. Jaguar '100'

24. I managed to own a '1½', but the '4·2' will elude me

*In which I change course*

became obvious to me when I came to strip down the Minor's engine, a job I felt I must do in my own interests, its previous owner having a rather less than delicate touch when operating his lathe, and I fearing that he may also have leaden feet, and that the little engine may have suffered. However, all was well.

Those engines had, because of their very compactness, minimal distances between their bearings, and plenty of bearing area. The overhead camshaft was driven by an odd arrangement, from the crankshaft, through two sets of bevel gears via the armature shaft of the vertically mounted dynamo. Odd arrangement it may have been, but the result was a degree of valve-timing accuracy which has probably not been equalled by any subsequent method. And certainly in the case of the Midget – if not the Minor – ability to sustain power at high revs could be attributed to this lay-out. The only snag was that owners often experienced trouble from oil finding its way from the valve gear to the dynamo windings, and thus 'losing their electrics'.

Having re-ground the valves, decoked the engine, reassembled it and given the body two coats of brushed black enamel, I was motoring again, going farther and farther afield at the weekends as confidence in the little bus grew. My only complaint was of a rumble from beneath, a rumble which suggested that the propshaft was out of balance. But it grew no worse and I did not trouble to investigate.

Until the intervention of the motor-bike – the period which Bunny had been pleased to call my 'lapse' – I had been teaching her to drive in the Swallow, and now, with the arrival of the Minor, we could resume our lessons. She was doing well, only the matter of reversing causing her much concern, so one Saturday afternoon we went along the quiet coast road near Crossens determined that the reversing manœuvre should be practised until she had complete confidence in herself. Practice we did, and confidence was on its way, when suddenly, she let in the short-travel clutch with a jerk, and things happened.

The Minor had a very pleasant arrangement, whereby each rear

*'Auto'-Biography*

seat foot well, on either side of the prop-shaft tunnel, had a wooden trap door which one could lift to gain access to the springs and shock absorbers, thus obviating crawling beneath. And when Bunny let her clutch in too quickly, one of these access hatches flew up into the car striking me a glancing blow and landing on the rear seat. Staring into the now opened hatchway, I saw the rear end of the prop-shaft resting on the road, a torn section of its fabric universal still adhering to its three-pronged spider. There was the cause of my rumble and the reason for the imbalance. My diagnosis had been right, but my inspection sadly lacking, for it was obvious when I examined the torn universal that only three of the six nuts and bolts had been holding things together, and that the jerk on the transmission had caused a complete severance.

I had no spare, this being a component to which one gave little thought, but we arrived home safely. By the simple expedient of bolting the two spiders solidly together, and dispensing with a flexible universal, I drove home, trusting to luck that no undue strain would be put on the shaft.

With the fitting of a new fabric disc the transmission was smoothed out beautifully, and the rumble vanished. And, although that Minor had seen many owners in its lifetime, and was probably on its second 'continuation' registration book, I now had sufficient confidence in it to consider a long run, and the venue I had in mind was, once again, Brooklands.

It was in 1937 when motor racing gained a boost; Crystal Palace being opened, Donington's circuit lengthened and a new circuit built within the confines of Brooklands itself – the Campbell Circuit. And the first race on this new circuit was planned for May 1st, the Campbell Trophy. This was one excuse for wishing to go down, the other being to watch a rising new star in action, the Siamese Prince Birabongse who raced as 'B. Bira', and who, in 1935 and 1936, had come out into the limelight driving Rileys, MGs and two ERAs called 'Romulus' and 'Remus'.

Bunny and I travelled through the night, the Minor getting us safely to Weybridge very early on the Saturday morning. At a

*In which I change course*

decently civilized hour I telephoned Peter Shaw's uncle, asked if I could prevail on his generosity again, and used his influence to gain access to the pit area of the Campbell circuit.

Students of motor-racing lore should read *History of Brooklands Motor Course* by William Boddy, editor of *Motor Sport* a splendid book, the reading of which brings the place back to life again. It is sufficient for me to give a brief description of the circuit within the circuit which bore the name of Campbell.

The primary consideration in the minds of the designers, was good visibility for spectators, and in this they certainly achieved their object. From Members' Hill almost the entire circuit could be seen, and, above the long row of concrete pits was a balcony, an idea borrowed from continental circuits such as the Nürburg Ring. The circuit itself was a mixture of old track and new road, with fast stretches along the banking and the Railway Straight, and with a new road paralleling the Railway Straight, which, after crossing the River Wey and after a sharp left-hand turn, cut diagonally across the old finishing straight and past the pit area. Whether the Campbell circuit could truly be described as a road circuit is subject to some doubt, but it was certainly interesting and measured 2·267 miles.

The inaugural race we had come to watch was run by the Brooklands Automobile Racing Club, and was for 100 laps, a total distance of some 226 miles, and, on a day which, though cold, was bright and sunny, we certainly saw some thrilling and brilliant driving.

Twenty-two cars lined up at the start, and perhaps if I listed just some of the drivers and cars, I will stir memories amongst some of my generation, and remind those who are younger of some of the 'greats' of the pre-war scene.

| | |
|---|---|
| B. Bira | Maserati |
| E. K. Rayson | Maserati |
| C. Brackenbury | Alfa-Romeo |
| C. S. Staniland | Alfa-Romeo |

*'Auto'-Biography*

| | |
|---|---|
| A. Powys-Lybbe | Alfa-Romeo |
| C. J. P. Dobson | Riley (Freddie Dixon's) |
| A. Dobson | Alfa-Romeo 'Bimotore' |
| Raymond Mays | ERA |
| Earl Howe | ERA |
| D. H. Scribbans | ERA |

There were twelve others, of assorted skills and with assorted transport, all of whom contributed towards the success of the Campbell Trophy Race, which was won by Bira's Maserati, after a stirring duel with the ERA of Earl Howe. Howe himself, glancing behind him for a fraction of a second as his car crossed the river bridge, lost his concentration and crashed into the parapet. The car was hurled into the air, landing partially on top of its driver, who suffered serious injury. Second was Rayson's Maserati and third Powys-Lybbe's Alfa-Romeo. Italian cars had a field day.

After the race, Peter's Uncle Harry positively refused to allow Bunny and me to start the journey home, insisting, not only that we had dinner with him, but that we stayed the night. The following morning, before leaving, I took Bunny into the garage to look at the Bentley I had driven around Brooklands, and, parked alongside it in the garage, was Peter's J3. Somehow, I felt much happier. It had indeed found a good home.

Because Chamberlain still had to wave his umbrella at us and assure us of peace in our time, there were signs within the Brockhouse factory – and of course in many others – that someone in Britain felt we should pull up our socks, and look to our defences; that the activities of the little man in Germany – the one with the comic moustache – and those of his Italian chum – the one with the chin – could just possibly be boding us no good. The signs manifested themselves in new blueprints bearing the unmistakable stamp of 'War Department' and in the tooling up of machines for the production of entirely new work. Surveyors bearing poles and theodolites could be seen wandering around the open ground

*In which I change course*

near the factory, suggesting that extensions were to be made. It was all very interesting, and certainly the increased activity helped the tradesmen of the town, for, although pay packets were small, more people were taking one home.

The £5 Minor continued to serve me well, taking me and two colleagues to and from work each day, and, at the weekends Bunny and I used it to go to as many beach race meetings, circuit meetings and scrambles as our limited resources would allow.

Suddenly, it seemed, twelve months had gone by, and it was the spring of 1938. In June, I went AWOL from the factory for three weeks, and had I, on my return, told Willie and certain of his cohorts just how those three weeks had been occupied, I am quite sure they would have bared their teeth, snarled, and called me 'a bloody capitalist'. As it was, I let them believe I had been 'missing – presumed sick'.

The fact is that I went to New York, saw some of it briefly, and came home again – and the trip did not cost me a penny. This was one of the better things which life occasionally hands out amidst the slings and arrows, and I suppose I should have taken greater advantage of it. But it was all so quick, and I was so unprepared.

I went out to accompany, and to deliver safely into his daughter's keeping, an old friend of the family, to whom a lifetime of hard work had brought high monetary reward, but whose health had suffered badly in the process. Although we tried to assure him that the shipping companies really looked after people well, he insisted that I go with him, and he footed the entire bill.

Because my stay ashore was limited to four days, I gained only a very hazy impression of that city of enormous buildings and its people, and, of my experiences during that visit, only two made any real impact, one of which, indirectly, was to result in me driving many thousands of miles in my own country.

Collected at the pier by Mr Laing's daughter and her husband, we were conveyed to their home in the Garden Suburb of Long Island, where our friend was to live out the rest of his days. And it was the conveyance which made the first impact on me, a Buick 'sedan', the first American-built car to come my way. On neither crossing, to or from the US, did I suffer any qualms or queasiness, but during my ride in that Buick and in other American cars during the next day or so, I felt positively sea-sick. Accustomed as I was to the firm ride of British cars, I found the American interpretation of good suspension very distressing, the long, slow pitching effect being similar to that experienced in a dinghy when a swell is running. And I have had no great liking for, nor much interest in American cars since that first introduction to them.

The second impact was made when Mr Laing's son-in-law took me to Battle Creek, the centre of the activities of the General Foods Corporation of America, for whom he worked. Here, in the enormous car parks I was delighted to spot several TA Midgets – those of the long-stroke 1292 c.c. engines, and pushrod-operated overhead valves – dotted amongst the massive and much over-chromed American cars. But it was when I was shown around the plant, and saw row after serried row of packaged foodstuffs, all destined for export to Britain, that the first stirrings of doubt came to me; doubt as to whether my decision to choose engineering rather than food as a career, had been the right one. There were cases of Post Toasties, Instant Postum, Certo, Jello, Maxwell House Coffee, Grape-Nuts, and many other products, and I learned that they would be handled by the Grape-Nuts Company which operated in my own country, information of which I made a mental note.

Home again, and back at my job, I was, perhaps inevitably after such an experience, unsettled and feeling very hemmed in by my surroundings. And, as Bunny and I were by this time beginning to think of marriage, it was an unfortunate time to be feeling indecisive. But, through one of the chains of circumstances, or coincidences, by which my life seems to have been governed, the issue was settled. I mentioned the name of the Grape-Nuts Company at Bunny's home one evening, and her aunt quietly remarked that their sales manager was a personal friend, and that he lived in Southport. I wrote a letter and in due course received a questionnaire in a format undoubtedly American. Three interviews

*In which I change course*

followed, each of them leaving me with the impression that I had been grilled by MI5 and, in a matter of three months, Bunny and I were married and, having sold the faithful Minor for £7 10s – thus showing a profit – I found myself representing the Grape-Nuts Company and driving a 'company car'.

One could recognize one's position in the hierarchy of the vast General Foods Corporation complex, by studying the large, printed 'family tree' presented to each newcomer. On this sheet of stiff card, which was headed 'Umpteen Thousand Stockholders' and then proceeded downwards through countless names, in order of importance, I found my own position, tucked away in the bottom right-hand corner – in the smallest possible print, and the very last on the sheet.

And one knew one's position in the British subsidiary company by the car one drove. Juniors had Austin 10s, seniors Austin 12s, area managers Austin 14s, and somewhere, in the misty upper stratas, there were Rovers.

There followed twelve months of most intensive motoring, during which 36,000 miles were clocked up by my Ten. As a member of 'The Flying Squad', a team of young reps, whose task was to call on every possible outlet for the products of our employers, I traversed the entire length and breadth of the British Isles. And it was all tremendous, and well-paid fun; a time when newspapers and radio talk were ignored, and the possibility of impending war only a very remote thing in the background.

It was a time when publicity gimmickry became fatuous – as it still is today. A time when, if the rival concern of Kelloggs gave away a toy balloon with its cornflakes, then we would give away a comic face-mask with our Post-Toasties; if they reduced their product by a halfpenny then we would reduce by one penny.

Bunny and I always said that our honeymoon was paid for by the Grape-Nuts Company. At a sales conference in Glasgow, a map of Scotland was torn up into sections, and I was handed one of them with the instruction that I must call on every shop in that area. When I studied my section I found that the luck of the draw

## 'Auto'-Biography

had given me the whole of Argyllshire and the Western Isles, and I had two weeks to spend in this glorious part of the country. As it was company policy to encourage wives to accompany their husbands on protracted journeys and during long absences from home – and indeed to pay half their expenses – I sent a telegram to Bunny which she has retained through the years and which is on my desk as I write: 'Leave Southport 9.50 Friday stop leave Glasgow Saturday morning 8.0 stop meet you Oban 12.30 stop send for your clothes later.'

Little wonder it caused so much hilarity back in Southport.

Dunoon, Inverary, Tarbert and down that wonderful scenic road along the Atlantic seaboard to Campbeltown. The lochs, the Clyde steamers to Arran and Bute. Life was good, and continued to be good in the months which followed, months when we lived in Edinburgh, Hull, Leeds, Bristol and London, and, at the weekends with good friends and colleagues, we watched as much motor sport as we possibly could.

The last Shelsley – won by Raymond Mays in a time of 37.37 seconds in his ERA – and the last, the very last Mountain Circuit Race at Brooklands, which, due to needing the services of a dentist urgently, I had to leave before the finish, and thus miss seeing my old friend Billy Cotton win it in an ERA.

And suddenly it was September 1939, and the whole world changed.

CHAPTER ELEVEN

# Sorting the wheat from the chaff

Soon after the outbreak of war the company ceased operations. Shipping now had sterner tasks to perform than the conveying of Post-Toasties to the breakfast tables of Britain, so our briefcases and our order books were stowed away, our cars disposed of and, with a promise of a reunion 'when it's all over' we all went our different ways, most of us offering our services to the war effort in one way or another.

My own offer was spurned with some such remark as 'Don't call us, we'll call you'. It seemed that the violent collision between my skull and the oven door handle so many years earlier, had done my optical department no good at all, and my eyes were considered unsuitable for the purpose of firing shots in anger. Strange that those same eyes should subsequently be found adequate enough to cope with the reading of micrometer and vernier gauges, and the setting up of machine tools to produce work to very fine tolerances. For, in due course, I found myself back at Brockhouse and now in charge of a long row of turret lathes, each operated by a woman.

And shall I ever forget those women? The Hon 'Sue' who handled a lathe with the same dexterity as she had a cocktail glass; Alice, with the vocabulary of a fishwife and heart of gold; Phyllis, the one with religion and a heart of stone, and 'Bet', our nympho who found an entirely new use for the machine shop air-raid shelters. These, and many more like them, all working interminable hours, often to the point of exhaustion.

Occasionally during those years I found myself back at the

wheel of a car, but always on authorized business and always limited by a strict allowance of petrol. A car took me to Windermere, on the shores of which Short Brothers were building and servicing their Sunderland flying boats. The window of the study from which I now write looks out over the bay where I was shown the art of 'unsticking' these heavy but beautiful aircraft from the surface of the lake, and returning them to their watery 'runway'. And a car took me to a bomber base from which I was shown how the Frazer-Nash gun turrets, which Brockhouse were producing, operated in practice. But the shots from those turrets over the Irish Sea, and those from a Home Guard Browning machine gun, with which I killed nothing but a rabbit on the Southport sandhills, were the closest I ever came to active service.

I met friends on leave, and we played golf and rock-climbed, promising ourselves good times to come. And when news of the deaths of some of these friends began to filter through, and news came of brother Tommy's commission somewhere out in Burma, I tried to break out and to join the newly formed REME. But to no avail – I was hauled back and told to get on with my job.

As an aspiring writer I was delighted when, one day, Air Commodore Hearson, our general manager, introduced me to one who had long been a firmly established man of letters, Compton Mackenzie. He was touring the firm's many factories seeking copy for his forthcoming book *Brockhouse*, and I like to think that to some small degree I contributed towards the success of that book.

We did not escape entirely unscathed. One night a Dornier, no doubt on his bombing run to nearby Liverpool, discovered our factory and presented us with a stick of its cargo, killing an apprentice and demolishing a tool-room. It was an incident which served to remind us that we were all in this thing together, and perhaps it eased a few uneasy consciences.

The Manchester factory with which father was concerned was also a target for bombs, which razed it completely, and although he was due to retire father joined us at Brockhouse, to serve again in the factory he had known and loved for so many years. When,

*Sorting the wheat from the chaff*

some months later, he died, he exhibited the precision so typical of him by leaving us at four o'clock on the fourth morning of the fourth month, 1944, and the large numbers of people from all walks of life, attending his funeral, testified to the esteem in which he had been held.

With the end of the war in Europe came a salutary reminder that peace was with us again. The lathes which for so long had been busy producing intricate components for aircraft and gun-turrets, were set up to produce pots and pans for use on electric cookers. A welcome change, but an anticlimax. It was time once more to seek the open road.

If I had accepted the offer made to me, I should probably now be writing the history of a travelling salesman, instead of a book about the cars in my life. For, true to their promise the Grape-Nuts Co asked me to rejoin them. But there was a snag which deposited me right in the centre of cross-roads, wondering which to take. The American parent company had taken over the British firm of Alfred Bird, to gain ready-made outlets for their products which were now to be made in this country, and they wished me to be based on Birmingham. Reluctantly I turned down their request. My degree of gregariousness is limited and I have an intense dislike of huge conurbations. The very thought of living and working in a vast industrial city was sufficient to make me thank my erstwhile and very friendly employers – and to turn in another direction.

When offered a job with another old-established firm which operated from the midlands; a job which promised me a large slice of the northern counties as my territory, I took it, and the Series 'E' Morris which went with it. And, prices of cars being phenomenally high at that time, I was quite content that mine should date back to 1939.

Introduced just before the war, the Series 'E' represented a startling leap forward in design. The logical successor to the Minors and Eights, it seemed to skip a few models in the process of evolution.

### 'Auto'-Biography

Gone were the running boards, resulting in a much wider car than the Eight; gone the traditional-looking radiator, replaced by a curved grill, and gone the mounted headlamps, now they were built into the wings and followed their contour. The boot was of usable proportions, and passenger space, fore and aft – although cramped by today's standards – was remarkably good. Still powered by the side-valve engine which had powered the Eight (and still cursed by a six volt system of 'electrics') it was quite possible to tune these cars until they could show most other eights a clean pair of heels.

My 'E' had been stored away during the war years and stored in a sensible manner, in that instead of being cocooned in various wrappings the air had been allowed to circulate around it. When I took delivery the little car looked immaculate, and its recorded mileage was a mere 9,000. All very promising and when my first run suggested that perhaps a little more acceleration would be desirable, I lost no time in getting to work on it.

A few thou. shaved off the head to raise the compression; a decoke, and new valves, nicely bedded to their seatings; a set of Terry's double 'Aero' springs, and the little engine was transformed. The tail-pipe was then replaced by one made of copper and of slightly larger diameter, which gave the exhaust note that beautiful resonance which only copper can give.

The increase in performance immediately showed up the faults of the cart-spring suspension which I gaitered with oily leather strapping. The Armstrong shock-absorbers which had not taken too kindly to years of inaction were replaced with Andre friction types, adjustable by spanner. A lot of fuss about a mere Series 'E', wasn't it? But, almost overnight it seemed, that car became a baby 'Gran Turismo' with that wheel at each corner feeling and a tautness which inspired confidence.

Obviously the first car to turn up, after years of deprivation, must have been a winner in my estimation. The Series 'E' just happened to come along.

In those days I had a certain colleague – one whom I used to call

*Sorting the wheat from the chaff*

friend until, in later years, he was tried and found sadly wanting. One of the group with whom I climbed and played golf, he too returned to the road at the end of the war, and bought himself a car identical to mine. But the similarity confined itself to their looks, for the performance of his was deplorable. We covered the same territories and so arranged our journeys that we could share our cars alternately and thus eke out our petrol rations.

After I had given my car 'the treatment' he was so depressed at the difference in the power of the two engines, that I decided to deal with his in similar fashion. I was happy with the result and felt that 'GUM', which was his car, was now equally as good as 'FOH', which was mine. But he would have none of it, and I am sure he felt I had deliberately skimped on something in order to retain the edge on him. I had skimped on nothing, but when I look back on those days, and remember that I, with my number two iron, could outdistance his number two down the fairway, I realize that technique must have had something to do with it.

Pity about that chap. While our friendship lasted he was damned good fun. But there we are, friendships should be able to withstand any acid test.

For many thousands of miles, FOH served me well. An economical and speedy means of transport for a traveller, and an ideal family car. For Bunny and I now had 'the kids' whom we would deposit on the back seat and set off for picnics, happy in the knowledge that the Series 'E' had only the two doors, and that there were no handles for exploring hands to find.

I shall never forget the one occasion when the little 'bus did let me down, and I sit shivering at my typewriter now as I think of it. Called to a sales conference at Nottingham, in bleakest midwinter, I left home early in the morning and drove to a colleague's home in Cheshire. From here we both drove down to the factory in his Morris Ten, lunched with the directors in the board-room, had our conference and returned to his home. Fortified by an excellent dinner, and just before midnight, I set off in FOH for my journey home, having telephoned Bunny to say I was on my way.

'Auto'-Biography

There was no heater in the car, but the last brandy was still functioning satisfactorily, and I was happy enough, musing to myself that I should have made a much better sales manager than the one who had been dictating policy to us that day. I was taking a short cut, along a winding country lane which would, I knew, lead me to the East Lancashire road and a fast run home, when my throttle foot went down to the floorboards and the car, all power gone and with its engine merely ticking over, coasted to a stop.

After long seconds of sitting and pondering, realization dawned that I had lost my throttle linkage; that I could no longer communicate my wishes to the engine, and with the realization came a reminder that for the last few miles the screenwipers had been fighting a losing battle against snow, that it was dark out there and that I had no torch. Obviously if I wished to get home I must apply the Heath Robinsonian part of my mind to the problem, and come up with an answer.

I decided that I needed string, and I had no string. I needed light, and I had no light. But there was a cottage of sorts across that field, a glimmer of curtained light told me so. I groped my way to the cottage to be greeted by a snarling dog, and an equally snarling human who wished to know "'oo the 'ell that was at this time o' night?"

Explanations given and reasonably good relations established and I had my string, and the loan of a cycle lamp, the battery of which was exuding that particular horrible substance exuded by ageing batteries, and which always finds its way to the outer casing.

The faint gleam from the lamp confirmed my suspicion that the soldered end of the Bowden throttle cable had come adrift, and that there was insufficient cable for me to tie it to the throttle lever. So I tied my string to the lever, opened the windscreen (bless that opening windscreen of the Series 'E') and fed the rest of the string through into the cockpit.

Returning the lamp to the still suspicious cottager, I set off for

*Sorting the wheat from the chaff*

home with the string wrapped around my right forefinger, thus activating the throttle through the screen and the small gap between bonnet and bulkhead. And what a journey that was. Forty miles in a blizzard, freezing hard and with an open windscreen. I was reminded of the ditty which ends 'it blew, it frew and then it snew, and then by jeez it friz', and I was very tempted to emulate the brass monkey by knocking at the door of the first blacksmith I came across to ask him if he did welding.

Bunny told me that when I eventually arrived home, at three o'clock that morning, I was semi-comatose and that the icicles which were suspended from my eyebrows had to be seen to be believed. I certainly remember that the forefinger which had driven my eight horses home took twenty-four hours to uncurl.

The intervention of war had done nothing to lessen my interest in motor sport, but as far as racing was concerned the immediate post-war years found this country bereft of circuits and sufficient petrol. There was racing in Europe, and the pages of *Autocar* and the other motoring journals kept all enthusiasts aware of the fact. And at home there were meetings at such make-shift circuits as Gransden Lodge airfield, and hill-climbs at Shelsley, Prescott, Bouley Bay and Rest-and-be-Thankful, all venues which now seemed – due to family, business and writing commitments – to be out of my reach. It was only a temporary phase and I was to make up for it later, but at the time it was all very frustrating.

There was one extravagant week-end arranged when, after carefully setting up a sequence of trusty baby-sitters, Bunny and I and two close friends planned a trip to Ireland in the September of 1949, to watch the Wakefield Trophy race for formula libre cars at the Curragh Circuit, Co Kildare. Fortunately, at the last minute our plans came unstuck. Fortunately because apparently there was a bit of a shambles at the start of the race, when a multiple crash, caused by slippery conditions, eliminated the entire front row of the grid. Because the field was now so depleted, the race, planned for twenty laps to give a total of 99 miles, was reduced to half distance and the interest was sadly diminished.

## '*Auto*'-Biography

Anthony Powys-Lybbe, whom I had last seen before the war at Brooklands, won the race in an Alfa-Romeo 'Monoposto' at a speed of 71·82 m.p.h. Not bad on a circuit the normal use of which was for army manœuvres.

Before leaving 1949 it is perhaps worth noting that the final points for the British Hill Climb Championship that year were, first Sidney Allard (3700 c.c. Steyr-Allard) with 39 points, second Dennis Poore (3·8-litre Alfa-Romeo) with 34, and in third place a new name appeared amongst those which were better known, that of a certain Stirling Moss (996 c.c. Cooper-JAP) with 30 points.

In 1950 I began to have the first uneasy feelings about the financial health of the company I was representing, and it became apparent that certain of my colleagues were experiencing the same unease. However I was assured by some of them who had been with the company for many years, that as soon as the young chairman – who was still serving out his time with the army – returned to take up the reins, matters would improve. So, although not at all happy about the policies of the caretaker management, nor about some of the products they were asking us to sell, I decided to do nothing precipitate, although plans for a future as a complete freelance were beginning to germinate in my mind.

I went to Earl's Court to do my stint on the company's stand at the British Industries Fair, and there, in the Tavern, an old friend introduced me to Donald Campbell. He was taking time off from problems concerning his father's old boat 'Bluebird', with which he was hoping to lift Sir Malcolm's world water speed record – 141·74 m.p.h. gained on Coniston Water in 1939 – safely beyond the reach of American contenders. After an hour of chatting of this and that, I left him and seventeen years later our paths were to converge again, when I was to write the book describing the last nine weeks of his life[1], and, two years later still, in collaboration with his mother Lady Campbell, I wrote his biography[2]. It's a strange old world, isn't it?

[1] *With Campbell at Coniston.*
[2] *Donald Campbell*, C.B.E.

*Sorting the wheat from the chaff*

I also attended, with Bunny, a sales conference which was held in Cornwall, a lavish affair designed to mark the return of the chairman, and perhaps intended to restore the now obviously sagging morale of the sales force. No businessman myself, and having an acute, though sympathetic perception of this same failing in others (I don't know, though, is it a failing?) I perceived in this conference much evidence of overspending, which only served to increase the unease I had been feeling.

A change of sales manager, very soon after we had all returned to our respective territories, did nothing to improve matters, and I decided to hand in my notice. The thing I most regretted was the parting with FOH, a faithful steed for which I and my family had developed a keen affection. But my move was the right one, for quite soon after I left them to enter a new phase, my fears proved justified and they ceased operations.

The spivs had been abroad in Southport for some time. Sharp boys, who had prospered from shady black market transactions during the war and its subsequent years of shortages, had turned their shabby attentions towards the demand for motor cars. Back street 'salesrooms' began to mushroom in the seedier parts of the town, cars in various states of disrepair were brought in from other towns, thick oil was poured into sumps and differentials, rust holes were camouflaged with filler, bodies given a cheap, quick 'blow-over' with cellulose, tyre faults filled with Bostik and the tyres themselves painted black. Then, when thousands of miles had been 'deducted' from speedometer readings (and these boys knew how to deal with either Smith or Jaeger) and when oil gauge needles had been slightly bent and thus made to show a more optimistic pressure, the cars were ready to show a handsome profit, and found no lack of buyers.

I had been pondering for some months over this strange market consisting of people willing to buy cars from other than well established and respectable sources, and I felt there was room for someone to try to counteract the activities of the wide boys. If this market was there to be tapped, then it should be tapped honestly, and the buyers should be supplied with reliable transport.

So commenced a long and enjoyable period when many cars passed through my hands, when I provided work and no little profit for a good many people who specialized in different aspects of car restoration, and sold sound, well-restored and well-prepared cars to a rapidly growing clientele. The zenith of that period came when people sought my cars because I had been recommended by others, and when well-known dealers and distributors began to 'phone me and ask if I could find them such and such a car, and sent me cars with the request that I restore them, sell them and return a fair price.

I do not pretend to understand the psychology of it, but even today there are many people who prefer to scan the private sale columns of the *Sunday Times* and other papers, rather than the block 'ads' of the large firms. So it was in those years of the fifties, and it was with such as these that I dealt. I met many people whom I call friend today simply because, at one time, I found them the very car they were seeking, put right anything that was wrong and sold it to them at a fair price.

Some of my success stemmed from the fact that I operated from my own home, in a district inhabited by the upper echelons in business and the professions, a district which had an aura of solidity and integrity. Some of this aura brushed off on to my cars and human nature did the rest.

Two whom I am happy to describe as nature's gentlemen – hackneyed though it may be – were neighbours, their houses facing mine across the road; Roland Knowles (who is no relation, although we always feel that he should be) who was then an Alvis devotee, and 'George' Arabin-Jones, a 'Jag' man in those days when the description did not have its present unfortunate connotation. Both took a keen interest in my activities and both freely offered me the facilities of their large garages, an offer which was most acceptable during those years when I found myself – to paraphrase Mr David Scott-Moncrieff – 'a purveyor of horseless

*Sorting the wheat from the chaff*

carriages to the middle classes' – and when my stocks of Rovers and Jaguars were rather high.

It was George who set me my greatest challenge. We were browsing around one of the seedier sales yards one Saturday afternoon (for one never knew when a pearl might turn up amongst the swine) when he drew my attention to a very shabby-looking ss 'Jaguar' 100 of, we guessed 1937 vintage. It was a sad example of a model which had been the epitome of pre-war sports cars, and which had been successful not only because of its ability to exceed the magic 'ton', but because it had cost less than half the price of its contemporaries.

For the benefit of those who knew it not, it was a magnificent-looking car, of classical line, and with a performance which did not belie the promise of its looks. Long bonnet, extravagantly swept wings, enormous Lucas headlamps (called P.100s, I think) a chopped-off tail, slab tank, cutaway doors and twin aero-screens. The car had a 6-cylinder, push-rod-operated, overhead-valve engine of $2\frac{1}{2}$ litres ($3\frac{1}{2}$ in later versions) with a seven bearing crankshaft, and twin su carburetters. There was nothing unusual about its 104-inch wheel-base chassis, nor about its suspension on semi-elliptics at each corner, but the car was remarkably light and, once one became accustomed to its foibles, a delight to drive.

George and I sat in this one and mused. The wooden dashboard had faded and bleached, but still possessed its full complement of instruments. The speedometer registered a phenomenal mileage, but the gear lever had very little sloppiness. There was little free-play in the steering, nor abnormal travel on the brake pedal. The leather seats were faded and scuffed, but they were intact, as was the skeletal hood – when we managed to erect it. Although the carpets were *non est*, the car, surprisingly, had retained its tonneau cover. Externally the chrome was good, but the paintwork was beyond restoration.

The engine fired at once, but announced its firing with a fusillade of rattle from little ends, a rumble of big ones, and a thick cloud of blue smoke. Nevertheless a short run around the houses

## 'Auto'-Biography

convinced us that the car had possibilities, that basically it was sound, was screaming out for loving care and attention, and needed a good home.

'I'll buy it,' said George. 'You restore it, and we'll share the profits.'

So commenced the long and pleasurable task of giving that Jaguar the attention it deserved and of putting new heart into it. I entrusted the work of re-boring the scarred cylinders and the supplying of over-size pistons and rings to Tom Baines, a specialist of the old school, with a proper respect for metal and machinery. Despite the hammering it must have received the crankshaft had remained true and, with new big-end bearing shells and carefully reamered little-end bushes fitted, that department was considered satisfactory.

Leaving to Baines the fitting of new valves and springs, and generally breathing new life into the engine, I pressed on with the job of refurbishing the car itself, checking the suspension, the braking and the steering, and renewing anything which called for renewal. The dashboard was re-stained to a matt finish, carpeting and rubber matting was bought, cut and fitted, and then, puzzled as to the correct treatment for ageing leather, I took the risk of painting the seats with a substance called 'Nuagane', and was pleasantly surprised by the authentic finish resulting from the application of this plastic and pliable liquid.

Turning finally to the task of painting the car itself, I decided against the use of cellulose, and used another product I am happy to endorse – 'Valspar' enamel. For I brush painted that body, rubbed it down and brush painted it again, and the Valspar dried to a perfect coachpainter's finish, without a single brush mark, and, when further lustre had been added by an application of hard Simoniz wax, the seventeen-year-old car looked as good as new.

I know I have 'gone on a bit' about this particular car, but it seemed to be a job of restoration which afforded me much pleasure, and the result was so worthwhile. My one regret was that I never had the pleasure of running-in that virtually new engine. For,

*Sorting the wheat from the chaff*

after toasting the future health of a bride and groom at their wedding reception at George's home, I watched the young couple leave for their honeymoon in the ss, and found myself in possession of the groom's previous transport, a 1938 Morris Eight. Obviously some deal had been transacted behind the scenes, and when the Eight came to be sold, the resultant profit was very good indeed.

I used to find myself most reluctant to part with some of the cars which passed through my hands, and certainly that ss was one of them.

One or two of the many who – with varying degrees of honesty – operated in the town during the fifties, managed to outgrow their lapses of the 'dodging and botching' period, and survived to open showrooms away from the back streets, where they now compete with the old-established firms in complete respectability. But if, as they sit behind their executive desks, gazing out at their stocks of 'low mileage, one owner' cars and watching their brash young salesmen at work, they could be persuaded to talk of those earlier days, motoring history would be enriched.

Although I am essentially a free-lance, with a dislike of partnerships, I did – in order to have access to his well-appointed and well-staffed workshops and lubrication bays – enter into an arrangement with a certain character. But when I discovered that he was sanctioning the filling of empty Bluecol tins with a cheap imported anti-freeze of the same colour, and selling it to fellow golf club members at the Bluecol price, then our arrangement came to an end. I am no paragon, but there are limits.

Having thus lost the facilities of his garage, I then started to look around for premises of my own, premises now made essential by the expansion of my business, and, just as I was on the point of buying a well-equipped and well-sited place near the town centre, fate chipped in once more with yet another diversion.

CHAPTER TWELVE

# We take to the hills

I suppose I could stretch this narrative by a further fifty thousand words in describing the sixteen years which passed, between the time of which I wrote in the last part of the preceding chapter, and my commencing to write this, the final one. But matters concerning space forbid this, and I must condense my tale into vignettes and extracts.

My experience in the food trade was a major factor in my being asked to run an importing company which had, due to food rationing, lain dormant during the war and immediate post-war years. But this did not mean I must abandon the connections in the motor trade which I had carefully nurtured over the years, and I found myself, after veering from 'comestibles' to 'combustibles', so to speak, now combining the two.

During my years on the road, I had dealt with many wholesalers and importers, in the course of which I became friendly with the directors of one such company. They entrusted me with the purchase of their various cars, and with the disposal of those they were changing. That they were satisfied with the Jaguars and 'ZA' Magnettes I selected for them became obvious when they recommended me to customers of theirs, three brothers in Northern Ireland who, among other interests, ran a motor business. They were seeking a reliable source for the supply of good, used cars to their country – cars bearing English registration plates having, apparently, a certain cachet in Ulster, and obviously being worth the cost of shipping.

I recall that the first car I shipped across from Preston was an Austin 'Devon', in pristine condition and having done a very low mileage. The car, the price I charged them, and the price they

*We take to the hills*

subsequently received, so pleased my new clients that the Devon became the start of a long sequence of such transactions.

Austin Sixteens, those of the 'alligator' bonnets, were firm favourites among the country-dwelling clientele of the brother who ran the car business, and as he seemed to order these very frequently, it became necessary for me to call in the services of the local Austin agents, Hattons, in the persons of Angus Ker and 'Mac' McTeggart. And I am happy to make passing reference to the fact that these splendid fellows sold nothing but the best, and still do. They are now directors of a large group headed by the same Percy Stephenson who used to electrify spectators and fellow competitors when driving his Austin Sevens in the pre-war beach races.

At first, my meticulous methods of car inspection amused them. My 'hyper-selectivity' they called it. 'Just watch, he not only looks at them and drives them, he crawls underneath the damn things.' In due course, however, they entered into the spirit of the game, and it became a point of honour between us that any car we shipped to Northern Ireland should be 'spot on', and I am sure we made happy motorists of many Ulstermen.

One of the brothers crossed the water to 'vet' a Bentley which I was about to ship to them, and so began an association with three of the most delightful characters life has steered in my direction, and which was to last for eleven years. I was never destined to meet the other two brothers in person, but the number of hours we spent in friendly, good-humoured conversation on the telephone, across the Irish Sea and over that long span of years, must have been astronomically high.

Very soon after this association began I was offered the lease of an old and rambling farmhouse close to the sand-dunes and beaches of the Mersey estuary; a gem of a place where rabbits and squirrels played and pheasants queued up at the doors to be fed by hand; where we were lulled to sleep by the mournful clanging of the bell-buoys out in the shipping channel.

Good friends, Peter and Di Elder, keen motorists both, moved into a flat at one end of the house, and here we all hoped and

## 'Auto'-Biography

expected to stay for many years. Here, at the week-ends, our friends gathered and we messed around with cars as others mess around with boats, or set up cine-cameras around the grounds until the place looked like an Elstree set, and the films we produced would have done justice to Hitchcock.

At Trap Hill, as the house was oddly called, I was able to pursue my car activities in greater space and now with the added advantage of having a six-car garage and a workshop. And, as I look back over those years, I suppose that the only British car to escape my net was the Aston-Martin. I longed for someone to order one from me, or to send me one to sell, but it seemed that my clients – although they were keen enough on elderly Bentleys, newer Jaguars and even, on occasion, ageing Rolls – were never quite in the Aston bracket. Every other marque seemed to come to Trap Hill, either on its way to be delivered, or sent to be cleaned up, worked on, and sold. And each had its own especial peculiarity and tended to reflect the driving (and some personal) habits of its previous owner. Some of the *objets d'art* found beneath the back seats of some of those cars when they came to be cleaned up, had to be seen to be believed!

Personal cars during the Trap Hill years included a Wolseley 1500, which whetted my appetite for the Riley 1·5 which followed; a splendid little car with excellent power to weight ratio and a sparkling performance. Well worthy of the diamond badge, although that badge was just about the sole remaining 'true Riley' bit! I also had two Rapiers, but kept neither of them long enough to establish a friendly relationship. I liked their instrumentation, their performance and, at that time, their looks, but I remember that I detested their carburation.

I watched the emergence of unitary construction, the disc brake, the coil spring, the anti-roll bar, the trailing arm and the torque reaction arm. And I watched the arrival of the transverse-engined, front-wheel-driven, hydrolastically suspended cars, the formula which, as they also have my favourite rack and pinion steering, I have adopted for my own transport.

*We take to the hills*

The coming of the BMC 'Farinas' sounded promising on paper, and I looked forward to their arrival. When I did see them, I shuddered, my aesthetic taste deeply offended. I felt sure that Pinin Farina must have had tongue in cheek when he designed them for Britain, and, although time has mellowed them, shaved off some of their angularity and lowered their lines, I am still of the opinion that neither the MG octagon nor the Riley diamond should ever have been stuck on to these bodies. However, when one sees them in such considerable numbers, it is certainly suggestive that I am in a minority of one. And I should be the last to deny their complete reliability and longevity.

Because the exigencies of shipping and the need to have cargoes shifted quickly tied me to my desk for what, at times, seemed to be twenty-four hours a day. I was unable to watch the post-war motor-racing pattern emerging at Silverstone, Brands Hatch or Goodwood. But Oulton Park, in its setting of woodland and lake, and Aintree, in direct contrast with its industrial backcloth, were both near home and I watched as much racing on these two circuits as I possibly could

It was at Aintree that I had the pleasure of meeting Stirling Moss on that memorable day in 1957 when, after driving a magnificent race, and giving a wonderful exhibition of how to shorten laps by corner-clipping, he brought his Vanwall first across the line and thus drove the first British car ever to win a British Grand Prix. And it was at Aintree that Mike Hawthorn took time out from a busy day to 'gen me up' with information for a magazine article, an article which, due to Mike's untimely death on the Guildford Bypass, never saw the printers' presses.

I suppose I saw most of the post-war generation of drivers at one time or another. Certainly I was twice lucky enough to watch Jim Clark in action, driving a Lotus in Formula Junior races. The first time was at Oulton Park when, in April 1960, he won the race, and the second was during the same month at Aintree, when he crashed, with a stuck throttle at the very last corner.

But motor racing generally was now out-pacing me. The era of the small, sensitive Grand Prix cars had arrived; cars with tailored cockpits, massive tyres and skeletal suspensions; cars driven by the young products of the clinical, scientific age. And racing had now become very much a business, bearing little resemblance to the racing of the 'string and copper wire' period in which I grew up. The amateur had been elbowed out of the way by the professional and it was time for doddering middle-agers like me to step aside.

As a middle-ager however, I did not then step into the ranks of those who are continually 'panning' the new young generation of motor sport enthusiasts. And I still haven't done so, although I deplore the 'boy racer' with his 'go faster tape' and his bad manners. To such as these I would say 'join a motoring club, and join a good one'. I stress the word 'good', for we all know how certain clubs and sectors within the motoring fraternity tend to give motor sport in general a bad name, and during our stay at Trap Hill we were certainly given one example of this.

The Southport Motor Club had reformed after the war, with new faces, new ideas and new techniques. As beach racing was still denied to them (although it has now started again and is regaining some of its old popularity) they turned to rallying and 'autocross' with their Minis, their Anglias and their 'Spridgets'. One year they asked if they could terminate one of their rallies at Trap Hill. As it was to be a Guy Fawkes Rally with bonfire, fireworks and all the 'trimmings' and I had happy memories of the Hardknott Rally, held so many years ago, I readily agreed. Their rally was a success, was followed by others in subsequent years, and at the end of each one they cleared the grounds of every scrap of litter and every spent firework, and some few days later presented Bunny with sprays of flowers.

Obviously, news got around that this fellow Knowles must be a sucker for this kind of thing, for I was approached by another club, which shall remain nameless. They too wished to hold a rally and to finish it with a barbecue in our grounds. Having in mind the example set by the Southport club, I agreed.

## We take to the hills

They certainly had their rally and announced their arrival at Trap Hill with a fanfare of 'straight-through' exhausts and a blare of horns. And they certainly had their barbecue, and their beer and scotch, and their fun in the bushes. When they departed, without a word of thanks, the grounds looked like a municipal rubbish dump, with beer cans and paper soup cups strewn everywhere – even stuffed into the outside loos. Well – that killed it for the other clubs. We lost interest.

The arrival of the BMC 1100s occurred during the Trap Hill days, and I found myself owning just about the first of the MGs to be seen on northern roads, and experiencing that rare pleasure of driving a car on which, for a while, all eyes were riveted.

I had ordered one of the newly announced Morris 1100s from Richard Burrows, owner of Burrows (Westmorland) Ltd, a dealer in cars in the finest tradition, and a man for whom the commercial aspects of selling has done nothing to diminish his enthusiasm and respect for the cars he handles. Telephoning his sales manager, Bryan Richardson, one morning to ask about delivery, he suggested that perhaps in view of the news he had just received, I may like to 'hold my horses' and to wait for the MG version which would be coming along shortly. As my own grapevine had let me down badly on this one, I was duly grateful to Bryan, who accepted cancellation of the Morris and, in due course, delivered the MG.

During its running-in period, the car attracted much attention in the car parks at Oulton Park, and during the run home from one meeting it let me down, literally. Mysterious thumps and bangs issued from the rear quarters, suggesting unsecured doors or that the boot lid was open. They were caused by neither of these things, and, extremely puzzled I drove slowly home, cursing myself for having fallen for the blurb about the Moulton-Issigonis cocktail on which these much vaunted cars were suspended, and convinced that they had either left out one major ingredient or that the interesting one, alcohol, had evaporated.

Some time elapsed before I came up with the answer, which was in fact a perfectly simple one. The rear sub-frame mountings, consisting of metal, bonded to rubber, had sheared. This, for a time, became an all too familiar occurrence to owners until BMC caught up with it, and seemed to improve the bonding.

After this, and one or two other minor teething troubles, I never found cause to fault the 1100s (although I do complain bitterly about the propensity of their 'undercarriages' for attracting rust, and feel that complete under-sealing should be as standard on a new car as windscreen wipers) and they, and their improved derivatives, have been personal transport ever since.

The day I parted with that first, grey MG to Pete Elder, and replaced it with one in Connaught green, is remembered because it coincided with the news that we also must part with Trap Hill. I received a letter that day advising me that my lease could not be renewed; that the old house, its grounds and surrounding acres of asparagus fields, were to be sold. I could if I wished, however, save and preserve it from the 'depredations of speculators', by buying the house and its small estate for £20,000!

With great regret we were compelled to look elsewhere, and Trap Hill – except in memory – no longer exists. Where it stood for so many centuries, and in its grounds, now stand row after row of red-brick 'commuter units', and where rabbits and squirrels played and pheasants strutted, stand the 'Jags', the Zephyrs and the MGBs of the Liverpool businessmen. Such is progress, and we can only hope that Trap Hill's friendly ghost, 'Jonathan' – which opened doors for us and closed them behind us – has successfully adapted itself to one of these products of the modern builder.

So we left the plains and turned to the hills, where we now live overlooking the bay, on Windermere, which saw Segrave speeding to his death. Those same waters are now traversed by the mono-skiers of a new generation, and in that same bay where Sunderland flying boats were once moored, cabin cruisers now roll at their buoys, their owners week-ending in caravans sited where the hangars and assembly shops once stood.

And living here, in the summer months, is as good as any international motor show. For they all come, Americans, Europeans,

## We take to the hills

Japanese, wearing every code of number plate imaginable. But in the winter they leave us to enjoy our motoring on uncluttered roads. November brings the RAC Rally, when my younger son Tony and I drive up to the Grizedale Forest section, to watch the Moss-Carlssons and the Timo Maakinens come through; when the quartz-iodine lamps of the Saabs, the Mini-Coopers, the Lancias and the Fords stab the night sky and point the way to Wrynose and Hardknott.

(Memo to Mr Raymond Baxter. On the night you turned up at the Kirkstone Inn check-point, looking very groggy after crunching your shoulder trying to unditch your car in Grizedale, I telephoned the BBC and ITV to that effect. Between them they sent me three guineas and, Mr Baxter, sir, I feel I owe you a drink!)

The winter of 1966–67 was memorable, for this was when I spent nine weeks in the company of Donald Campbell and his team, watching them during the day overcoming problems against seemingly insuperable odds, and at night writing the book of the project against an urgent publishing deadline. Nine weeks when my little MG ran through a set of tyres as it chased across the fell roads to Coniston and back again each day, and when my feet almost went though the floor of the car as the rust started its pernicious work during that appalling winter. I noticed that Donald's blue E-type was looking none too happy at the end of those weeks.

We all expected that project to meet with ultimate success, and that my final chapter would tell how Campbell gained his newest record. We did not expect that the book would have to be speedily re-written, pitched in a lower key, or that the last chapter would be an eye-witness account of the manner in which he died.

Of all the correspondence I am now conducting with people in many parts of the world, as a direct result of the kind reception given to that book and to the biography which I later wrote with Donald's mother Lady Campbell, perhaps the most fascinating is that which has developed between Leonid Tregubenko of Leningrad, and myself, 'Lenty' is an engineer and editor with the

## 'Auto'-Biography

Russian magazine *Motor Boats and Yachts* and has an astonishing knowledge of motoring matters. His frequent letters to me, and my replies, are an example of how the gap between peoples of differing ideologies may be bridged by a common interest. The friendship with Lenty is one more for which I have to thank the motor car.

During the time between the publishing of those two books, I lost an eye, and with it, or so I thought, the ability to drive. Surgeons and specialists alike hinted that, as far as future driving was concerned, I had probably 'had it'. I was uncertain which was the worst, the loss of the eye or the end of a motoring life, and it was to take our family doctor, friend and sportsman, to put an end to that spot of depression.

'Put your black patch on,' he said. 'Get your car out and drive the damned thing. You'll soon adjust.'

He was right, and to prove his point, I entered for a driving contest organized by the Advanced Motorists' Association, and performed all their 'tricks' satisfactorily. Now, whenever I pass our local taxi-driver, who is similarly afflicted, we grin and call out 'Snap!'

Did I pass on to my brood any of my enthusiasm for cars? Well, my elder son, like my brother before him, sees in a car a mere accessory to life, or a subject for the cartoons he draws for the national press, and my daughter only insists that there be room enough in a car for three dogs, and in its boot for a bale of hay for her donkeys. So it was left to my younger son to carry on the tradition, and already he has had through his hands almost as many cars as I had, at his age. His personal fight against the rust has just been lost, and he is busy fitting a new rear sub-frame to his Riley 'Elf'.

As for my grandson; his collection of cars by Messrs Lesney looks distinctly promising. I only hope that when his turn comes to jostle for space on the overcrowded roads of these islands, he will manage to have some of the fun I have had with cars, and that, although those of his generation will be vastly different, at least the

*We take to the hills*

names on their badges may still be the same. I would have loved to think that my grandson's turbo-jet-propelled car may have even worn the diamond badge of Riley, but it now seems that the demise of this illustrious name is a *fait accompli*, and I can only, now, join in its requiem, by giving him for his future reading a brief history of this famous marque.

Although the life-span of the Riley motor-propelled vehicle was, as I pen these words, exactly seventy years, the first Riley car proper was designed by Percy Riley (one of the sons of the founder, William) between 1896 and 1898, and it employed, for the first time in car engine design, a mechanically operated inlet valve. Quickly, public favour was won, and the marque became a leader in the British light car field.

In trials, rallies and hill-climbs, and at Brooklands, Riley cars won international fame as they were driven by such men as Freddie Dixon, Malcolm Campbell, George Eyston and Raymond Mays, and from these cars stemmed saloons, tourers and sports cars bearing such splendid names as Adelphi, Alpine, Falcon, Redwing, Imp, Kestrel, Lynx, Monaco and Stelvio – cars which continue to be of abiding interest to the discerning.

Perhaps it may be said that the Riley was a car which 'died' twice, for in 1937 the company was in deep financial water. Fortunately Lord Nuffield stepped in and saved the day, and the name of Riley, by privately purchasing the company and later re-selling it to Morris Motors, who continued – as did their successors, BMC – to produce cars wearing the name of Riley, even if they did have most unRiley-like features.

Now, it would seem, death is final; that, in the interests of 'rationalization', there is to be no attempt at revival. However hundreds of pre-Nuffield examples still exist, tended with great affection by their owners, whose interests are well catered for by the Riley Register, the Riley Motor Club and the Riley RM Club.

Well, there we are. Some grim times, but generally speaking – and thanks mostly to the motor car – a lot of fun. Now I write

159

# 'Auto'-Biography

about them and, for my editors, review the writings of others who share my feeling for them. At the weekends our friends shoot up the motorways to join us, arriving in machinery both delectable and not quite so delectable. Rover 3500s, MGB GTs, Cortinas, Vitesses and Coopers. Each to its owner's taste, needs and pocket.

Last weekend we thought the Athenaeum Club had been transported to our door in the shape of a Jaguar XJ6 4·2-litre. All that polished wood and pleated leather, and the air of quiet opulence. And the whisper-smooth silence – spoiled only by the thin whine from the 'diff'.

Bunny and I watched it as our friends rejoined the traffic stream to glide south again in the evening, and then turned to our little Princess 1100, bought second-hand, with the first year's depreciation already off it (well it's the only way, isn't it?).

'Look', she said. 'Polished wood and pleated leather, and a thin whine from the transmission. And that idler-gear rattle you love so much!'

'Yes,' quoth I, 'and if someone would drop a 70 b.h.p. unit from an MG or Riley 1300 into that sub-frame, I would settle for that.'

And so I would – if I could keep the rust at bay. The comfort furnished by Vanden Plas would make due obeisance to the passing of the years, and the higher compression and changed gear ratios of the power pack (to say nothing of that long awaited and much welcomed 'synchro' to bottom gear) would satisfy the youthful sporting instincts which, I am happy to say, still linger.

We have most of the other variations on the theme, and we now have the 1300 GT, but down at BLMC they seem to have missed out on my particular permutation, which is a pity. For driving the fell roads – winter and summer – and for my own occasional sortie down the motorways, it would – at least for me – produce the finest small car of the decade which, like this narrative, is now coming to an end.

*Quarry Garth*<br>
*Windermere*<br>
*Feb.-Sept. 1969*

# Index

Advanced Motorists' Assoc., 158
Amalgamated Engineering Union, 127
Aintree Circuit, 153
AJS Motor-cycle, 119
Alvis car, 52, 146
Alfa-Romeo car, 32, 37, 74–75, 80
Amilcar, 32
Arabin-Jones, 'George', 146–7
Aston Martin car, 152
*Autocar*, 42, 82, 143

Baxter, Raymond, 157
Benjafield, Dr J. D., 124
Bentley, 'W. O.', 122
Bentley car, 42, 45, 53–54, 73, 85, 122
Birkin, Sir 'Tim', 49, 52
Birabongse, Prince, 130
Bouley Bay Hill-climb, 143
Bolster, John, 109–10
Boddy, William, 131
British Hill Climb Championship, 144
British Industries Fair, 144
British Leyland, 47, 82
B.M.C. 'Farinas', 153
British Electric Vehicles, 19–20
Brockbank, Harry, 121
Brooklands, 29, 31, 99, 120–2
Brockhouse (Southport) Ltd, 126, 128, 138

Brands Hatch Circuit, 153
Buick car, 134
Burrows, Richard, 155
Burrows (Westmorland) Ltd, 155
Bugatti car, 32, 52–53

Campbell, Sir Malcolm, 30, 32, 36, 38, 39, 49, 52, 54–55, 58, 61, 159
Campbell, Donald, 144, 157
Campbell, Lady Dorothy, 144, 157
Castrol oil, 57
Coatalen, Louis, 31–32, 37
Conelli, Count, 31
Cotton, 'Billy', 61–63
'Cortina', Ford, 160
Coniston Water, 144, 157
Crystal Palace Circuit, 130
'Continental' engines, 36
Clark, 'Jim', 153
Cunliffe, May, 40, 43, 45, 54, 57–58
Curzon, Lord, 52
Cushman, Leon, 52–53

Daytona beach, 54
*Daily Dispatch*, 55
Davenport, B. H., 45
Delage car, 32, 37
Dixon, Freddie, 123–4, 159
Dobson & Barlow Ltd, 115

161

# Index

Don, Kaye, 49, 52–53
Donington Park circuit, 130
Dunfee, Jack, 54

Earls Court, 144
Edinburgh, 28
E.R.A. car, 130
Elder, Peter, 151, 156
Elder, Diana, 151
Eyston, Capt. George, 96, 109, 159

Frazer-Nash car, 32, 45

General Foods Corporation, 134–5
Goodwood circuit, 153
Grizedale Forest, 157
Guinness, Kenelm Lee, 36

Hawthorn, Mike, 153
Hampson, 'Tom', 14
Hampson, 'Joe', 14
Hartley, Sir William, 26
Hartley, Christiana, 26
Harper-Bean car, 59
Halliwell, 'Vic', 67, 69, 71
Hardknott Pass, 86–87, 89, 90–91
Hardknott Castle, 86, 91
Hattons (Southport) Ltd, 151
Hearson, Air Commodore, 138
Hotchkiss engines, 36, 101

Irving Napier, 66
Issigonis, Sir Alec, 155
Isle of Man, 85

Jaguar XJ6 4·2 litre, 160
Jowett car, 100–1

Ker, Angus, 151

Kimber, Cecil, 96
K.L.G. spark plugs, 36
Knowles, 'Ernie', Chaps 1–11 inc.
Knowles, Capt. 'Tommy', 13, 15–16, 24, 40, 61, 73, 105–7
Knowles, Hilda 'Bunny', 80, 87–88, 101, 112, 129, 132, 135, 136, 141, 160

Leyland Motors Ltd, 15, 18, 59, 73, 76
Lea-Francis cars, 47–48, 49, 52, 59–60
Long Island N.Y., 133
Lurani, Count 'Johnny', 109
Lyons, William, 73

Masetti, Count, 31
Makinen, Timo, 90, 157
Martindale, 94, 98
Mackenzie, Sir Compton, 138
Mays, Raymond, 30, 45, 54, 58, 136, 159
McTeggert, 'Mac', 151
Mercedes cars, 45, 52–53
Meadows engines, 48, 50
M.G. Cars, 85, 96, 108, 120–1
MILLE MIGLIA, 108
Mitford, Nancy, 84
Morris, William, 35–36
Morris 'Bullnose', 34–36, 101
Morris 'Minor', 128, 133
Morris Series 'E', 139–42
Moss, Stirling, 144, 153
Moulton, Alec, 155
Moss-Carlssons, the, 90, 157
*Motor*, the, 42

National Trust, 91
Newtownards circuit, 50–51, 54
New York, 133

162

# Index

Nürburg Ring, 131

Olympia Motor Show, 41
Oulton Park circuit, 153

Pendine Sands, 36, 39
Phoenix Park circuit, 85
Posthumos, Cyril, 68
Prescott hill-climb, 143

Royal Automobile Club, 38, 85, 93
R.A.C. Rally, 157
Rest-and-be-thankful hill-climb, 143
Richardson, Bryan, 155
Riley cars, 42–43, 47, 80, 81, 82–84, 99, 159
Roots superchargers, 37–38, 74, 85
Rootes Group, 60
Rolls-Royce, 26, 42, 66
Rover cars, 135, 160

Segrave, Sir H. de Hane, 30–31, 36–37, 65, 67, 68–69, 71–72
Shelsley Walsh hill-climb, 43–44, 46, 54, 99, 108, 136
Shaw, Peter, 119–20, 121–5
Shuttleworth, Richard, 124
Silverstone circuit, 153
Southport Motor Club (pre-war), 29–30, 38, 40, 54, 58
Southport Motor Club (post-war), 154

Southport, 13, 15, 28, 37, 65
S.S. Jaguar, '100', 147–8
Standard car, 78–79, 81
Stewart, 'Bill', 85–86, 115
Stanton, 'Jill', 96
Spurrier, Henry, 15, 76
Sunbeam cars, 30–31, 36–37, 57, 65
Sunbeam-Talbot-Darracq, 31
*Sunday Times*, 146

Taylour, Fay, 108
Thomas, Parry, 39
Thistlethwaite, 'Scrap', 52
Tilling-Stevens, 60
Tregubenko, Leonid, 157–8
Triumph 'Tiger', 113, 117–19

Ulster Tourist Trophy race, 49

Vanwall car, 153
Vanden Plas, 160
Vauxhall-Villiers, 32, 57–58
Villa, Leo, 61
Vulcan Motors Ltd, 13–16, 47, 58–59
Vulcan car, 17, 22, 60

Walton, Ken, 90–91
Walmesley, William, 73
War Department, 14, 114
Wardman, C.P., 59
Windermere, 65, 156
Wilcocks, Michael, 67–68, 71
Wrynose Pass, 86, 89

163

## GEORGE ALLEN & UNWIN LTD

*Head Office*
*40 Museum Street, London W.C.1*
*Telephone: 01-405 8577*

*Sales, Distribution and Accounts Departments*
*Park Lane, Hemel Hempstead, Herts.*
*Telephone: 0442 3244*

*Athens: 7 Stadiou Street*
*Auckland: P.O. Box 36013, Northcote Central N.4*
*Barbados: P.O. Box 222, Bridgetown*
*Beirut: Deeb Building, Jeanne d'Arc Street*
*Bombay: 103/5 Fort Street, Bombay 1*
*Calcutta: 285J Bepin Behari Ganguli Street, Calcutta 12*
*Cape Town: 68 Shortmarket Street*
*Delhi: 1/18B Asaf-Ali Road, New Delhi 1*
*Hong Kong: 105 Wing On Mansion, 26 Hancow Road, Kowloon*
*Ibadan: P.O. Box 62*
*Karachi: Karachi Chambers, McLeod Road*
*Madras: 2/18 Mount Road, Madras*
*Mexico: Villalongin 32, Mexico 5, D.F.*
*Nairobi: P.O. Box 30583*
*Philippines: P.O. Box 157, Quezon City D-502*
*Rio de Janeiro: Caixa Postal 2537-Zc-00*
*Singapore: 36c Prinsep Street, Singapore 7*
*Sydney N.S.W.: Bradbury House, 55 York Street*
*Tokyo: C.P.O. Box 1728, Tokyo 100-91*
*Toronto: 81 Curlew Drive, Don Mills*

# DONALD CAMPBELL, C.B.E.
## ARTHUR KNOWLES AND DOROTHY, LADY CAMPBELL

This is the biography of a man who lost his life in the search for 300 miles an hour on water. Donald Campbell was an enigma to many people. A complex character, subject to many moods, 'one either loved the man or hated his guts'. Few could understand the obsessional drive which led him on to greater and greater effort and finally, in January 1967, to his tragic death; many who knew him only as a public figure had no idea of what Donald Campbell was really like. There is, however, one person qualified to write about him – his mother. Lady Campbell furnishes the details of Donald's childhood and family life with great warmth and without any kind of bias, and the rumour, speculation and misunderstanding which accompanied Donald so often in his lifetime are disposed of once and for all in a remarkably straightforward manner.

The technical information and stories behind the building of the Bluebird cars and boats are supplied by Arthur Knowles, engineer and motoring correspondent by profession, who has made a life study of motoring in all its aspects. Knowles spent nine weeks at Coniston with Campbell in 1967, and was an eyewitness to his death and readers will remember his previous book *With Campbell at Coniston*. His collaboration with Lady Campbell on this book has produced the first real portrait of Donald Campbell, a great man, patriot, and explorer in speed.

'... so different from previous books about Donald C or his father, Malcolm. Lady Campbell has provided letters and other material to add new interest to the legends of the Campbells. If you want to know more about this remarkable family this is one for you.' *Car Racing*

# BRITISH RACING GREEN
## ANTHONY PRITCHARD

Connaught, Vanwall, Cooper, Lotus – the cars that brought Grand Prix victories to Britain after years of apathy towards motor racing; the failure of the V-16 B.R.M.; Jaguar, the name which scored so many wins at Le Mans that the name became almost synonymous with the Twenty-four Hour race, and Aston Martin, winner of the Sports Car World Championship and the difficult Nurburgring 1,000 Km. race three years in succession. The names which have contributed so much to Britain's present dominant position in international motor racing are the principal players in this fascinating and carefully researched account of post-war British motor racing fortunes. *British Racing Green* is not only concerned with the cars that have secured for themselves a permanent place in motor-racing history, but also the gallant efforts of such teams as H.W.M., who in the early 'fifties appeared at a Continental event almost every week-end in the racing season, the sports car successes of Frazer Nash, Tojeiro, Lister and other small constructors, together with the early post-war Alta and E.R.A. Other chapters narrate the consistent performances of the B.R.M., the Anglo-Australian Brabham and the successes and failures of the various cars built by Elva and Lola.

This is a success story spread over twenty years of hard work and determination, and is told by a well-known motoring journalist and author who has an intimate knowledge of the British and Continental motor racing scene and who has himself experienced both the bitter taste of motor racing failure and the joy of success.

# THE GRAND PRIX CAR
L.J.K. SETRIGHT

After sixty glorious years of Grand Prix motoring, the latest cars are just twice as fast as those of 1906. Many of the most important and dramatic developments in racing cars took place between 1954 and 1966, the years covered by this book in which L. J. K. Setright continues the work of description and analysis begun by the late Laurence Pomeroy, whose two similar volumes finished at 1953. Since 1954, new car design philosophies, new engineering difficulties, new driving techniques and new environmental features have transformed the racing car; it is a feature of this book that all these influences are discussed in a measure that will not disappoint the engineer, and in a language that will not daunt the sportsman.

Here, in a quarter of a million elegant words and more than 150 informative illustrations, is the story of the most fertile and competitive era in the history of motor racing. A narrative section traces the technical developments by which the classical racing car reached its zenith and yielded to a new order. An analytical section probes deeply into the theories and technologies involved – into the chemistry of fuel, the intricacies of tuning, the mechanics of construction, the dynamics of cornering, and all the many other niceties of design. Finally, all important cars are examined in detail, their performances mathematically compared and their characteristics entertainingly contrasted.

# RETURN TO POWER
# THE GRAND PRIX CARS OF 1966
MICHAEL FROSTICK

For motor-racing enthusiasts, major changes in the power formula from 1,000 c.c. to 3-litres has given the year 1966 a unique interest. Michael Frostick, widely known for his highly successful collaboration with Richard Hough in several books, including *History of the World's Racing Cars*, has made a study of the effect of the new formula in all the principal events of the year. After filling in the background of some notable 3-litre cars in the past, he describes the European circuits, the cars and their drivers, the races in Europe and the Transatlantic finale.

'A topical and well-illustrated interim history of the formula's first two seasons.'
*The Sunday Times*

# A HISTORY OF THE HIGH PERFORMANCE MOTOR CAR
RICHARD HOUGH AND MICHAEL FROSTICK

An illustrated survey of the origins and development of the outstanding automobiles produced in Europe and America which have been designed for the fast driver and motoring connoisseur: the high performance motor car.
'A splendid volume dealing with the most glamorous fast cars since the birth of motoring.' the *Daily Telegraph*

# FIRST AND FASTEST
RICHARD HOUGH

Racing drivers and motoring writers bring together and make live again in this book some of the greatest motor races of the century – from the days when lofty giants of machines, handled by goggled giants of men, careered from city to city across the dusty roads of Europe, to the fastest race of all time, when Europe met America at the concrete speedway of Monza only five years ago. Each of these accounts marks a milestone in the timeless struggle towards new records in racing competitions: Bentley won five times at Le Mans; the struggle in 1930 was the keenest and fastest of them all. All through the 1920s the American Indianapolis drivers strived for the three-figure winning speed; only in 1925 did they achieve their goal. The Mille Miglia was never won at that magic target pace of 100 mph; in 1955 Stirling Moss came nearer to this unattainable goal than any man before or since, in the most remarkable sustained piece of driving in the history of motor racing. And so to the fastest race ever run at Brooklands, recounted by that erudite historian, W. Boddy; to that 160 mph battle-royal between Auto-Union and Mercedes at Berlin in 1937; and others. There is a chapter for all tastes and moods, and never a dull moment.

# A HISTORY OF THE WORLD'S RACING CARS
RICHARD HOUGH AND MICHAEL FROSTICK

The authors dig quickly into the nineteenth-century roots, tracing them through the Edwardian monsters to the main stream, from which flourished the great figures of the period 1911 to 1916: Ernest Henri, Ettore Bugatti, Fritz Nallinger, the Duesenberg brothers among them. The revival in the early 1920's brought about equally intense competition, rich technical progress, and unexpected successes by Britain and the U.S.A. in Europe's senior event. Then, with the growing specialization of American track racing, this brief history is broken by studies of the Indianapolis scene, with its unique compound of bustling energy, conservative development and daring innovation.

The rise of Fascism in Europe brought new standards, new techniques and new political implications to motor racing. The last half of the book, as richly illustrated and briskly recounted as the first, describes the dominance of science over traditional values, and the renaissance in recent years fed by the new enthusiasm of British, American and Japanese designers. On the eve of a new formula and a new golden age of motor racing, this is an appropriate time to look back to the origins and development of the racing car. With its wide range of superb photographs, this book provides a pleasurable and profitable way of doing so.

'... a useful (and very well written) "outline guide", tracing and illustrating the major landmarks in racing car design.' *Sports Car*